Geoffrey Oldfield is a retired local government officer who has been interested in the history of Nottinghamshire for many years. He has been able to combine this with his other interests, cycling and photography, to get to know and record many of the county's features.

He also contributes articles to a number of magazines and publications and gives talks to local history and similar societies.

Frontispiece
The summer house in the grounds of Kelham Hall (see No 50).

Nottinghamshire Curiosities

Geoffrey Oldfield

THE DOVECOTE PRESS

First published in 1992 by The Dovecote Press Ltd
Stanbridge, Wimborne, Dorset BH21 4JD

ISBN 0 946159 98 X

© Geoffrey Oldfield 1992

Phototypeset in Times by The Typesetting Bureau Ltd
Wimborne, Dorset
Printed and bound in Singapore

Contents

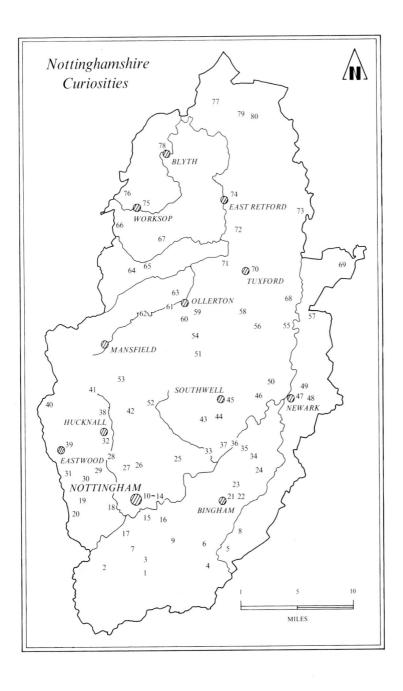

Nottinghamshire
Curiosities

N

77
79 80

78
BLYTH

76
75 74
WORKSOP EAST RETFORD 73
66
67 72

64 65 71 70
TUXFORD 68
69

63 OLLERTON
61 59 58
62 60 56 55 57

MANSFIELD 54

51

53 50
41 SOUTHWELL 49
40 52 45 46 47 48
HUCKNALL 42 43 44 NEWARK
38 32
39 37 36 35
EASTWOOD 28 33 34
31 29 27 26 25 24
30 23
NOTTINGHAM 10-14 21 22
19 18 BINGHAM
20 15 16 8
17 9 6 5
7 4
2 3
1

1 5 10
MILES

Introduction

In a poem published in 1948, entitled 'The Town Clerk's Views', John Betjeman wrote 'He was like all Town Clerks, from north of Trent'. Whether this is true or not, it illustrates the idea that northern and southern England are divided by the River Trent. Nottinghamshire can therefore claim to have a foot in both camps as the 'smug and silver' Trent divides the country into two unequal parts, the larger portion being the northern section. The geology of the two parts is different and this has influenced the history and character of them.

South of the river had until this century, apart from Newark, few urban areas and was, and still is, mainly agricultural. The fertile Trent Valley, the clays, part of the Vale of Belvoir shared with Leicestershire and a range of low hills, the wolds, contribute to a mixed farming area.

The county town of Nottingham just north of the river was a market town and regional capital for centuries and started to become industrialised towards the end of the seventeenth century. To the north and west of the town was an exposed coal-field, worked in a small way since the thirteenth century. When the stocking-frame industry came to the East Midlands, villages in the area became industrial ones, with hosiery and mining becoming larger scale in the nineteenth century.

Towards the north west of the county, the mainly lighter soil had produced Sherwood Forest, a royal hunting preserve which was later to be handed over to aristocratic owners, giving it the name The Dukeries.

Further to the north and over towards the north bank of the Trent was again mainly clay and good agricultural land, but like Sherwood Forest and The Dukeries less thickly populated than the south-west.

Some of these aspects of the county are reflected in the curiosities in this book. As in many other counties changes have taken place and are still taking place. Mining has moved eastwards, with newer collieries unlike in appearance above ground those that have disappeared. Industry is changing and becoming less obtrusive. The Dukes have gone and new uses found for their former estates.

Country parks and other facilities now provide for increased leisure and to attract tourists to what in the past was a county through which people passed. Some of the items in the book reflect these changes too, as well as some of the people, well known or not so, who have contributed to the variety to be found in the county.

Geoffrey Oldfield

Acknowledgements

Having lived in Nottinghamshire most of my life I have probably absorbed much of its history and topography in a number of ways. I am
grateful particularly to friends I have met through the Thoroton Society
of Nottinghamshire and the Nottinghamshire Local History Association who have, knowingly or unknowingly, contributed to my store of
information. I am indebted too to the resources of the Nottinghamshire
Archives Office and the Local Studies Libraries at Angel Row, Nottingham, and especially their ever helpful staffs.

My thanks are also due to my wife Freda who has typed the script
without complaining about my handwriting.

The school and almshouses at Bunny.

1 Contriving and Drawing All His Own Plans

Position: Bunny, 5½ miles south of Nottingham
O.S. Map: Nottingham & Loughborough area: Sheet 129: 1/50,000
Map Ref: SK 583/295
Access: On the A.60 road next to the church.

The words of the title were Sir Thomas Parkyn's own description of one of his many skills, that of an amateur architect. There are several examples of his designs in Bunny and in nearby Bradmore and East Leake. The school and almshouses are remarkable for their architectural features and illustrate another of his talents for he was also the author of a Latin grammar. Immediately over the door are the words 'Disce et discede' – learn and depart, whilst to the left and right are two inscriptions, 'Scienta non habet inimicum nisi ignorantem' – knowledge has no enemy but ignorance and 'Nemo hinc egrediatur ignoras Arithmetices' – no one leaves here without a knowledge of arithmetic.

Above the door is a panel which tells of the charitable works which he and his mother carried out for the good of the village. Above this is his coat of arms, and just to make sure that we are aware of who designed and paid for the building, also his initials and the date 1700.

Sir Thomas Parkyns, the first baronet, lived from 1662 to 1741 and trained as a lawyer. He was also something of a physician and collected stone coffins. He would like to be remembered for one of his other hobbies, that of wrestling, for he designed his own wall-monument in the church of St. Mary, where he is depicted about to start a wrestling bout.

Places of Interest in the Neighbourhood
The Men of Gotham – Foolish or Wise? (Gotham)
A Serious Offence was Committed (Bradmore)
A Clergyman's Invention Lives On (Ruddington)

2 The Men of Gotham – Foolish or Wise?

Position: Gotham, 5½ miles south west of Nottingham
O.S. Map: Nottingham & Loughborough area: Sheet No. 129: 1/50,000
Map Ref: SK 535/304
Access: The Cuckoo Bush public house is in the centre of the village, near the junction of the roads to East Leake and Kingston-On-Soar.

The sign at the Cuckoo Bush Inn depicts the villagers of Gotham building a hedge round a cuckoo so that it would remain there. They did this as they were intrigued by its song. This is just one of the legendary tales told about the 'Wise Men of Gotham'. Others that seek to ridicule their intelligence include the story of their trying to rake the reflected moon from a pond, thinking it was a cheese and of trying to drown an eel in a pond.

The Gotham stories are said to date back to the reign of King John in the early thirteenth century. According to tradition, the King and his entourage were passing through Gotham on their way to Nottingham. The villagers were convinced that if any royal person passed over land it became public property. They apparently tried various stratagems to deter the King's retinue from their land. The King later sent his officials to Gotham to punish the villagers for their interference. The villagers thereupon indulged in the various foolish practices ascribed to them, in the hope that the officials would consider them not responsible for their actions and so would not punish them.

The stories were no doubt handed down by oral tradition for generations until in the reign of Henry VIII they were written down by Andrew Borde. They were published as *Certain Merry Tales of the Mad Men of Gotham*. It is supposed that the term 'Merry Andrew' originates from this. The tales seem to have appealed to the unsophisticated for centuries thereafter and were frequently reprinted.

The name of the Nottinghamshire village is pronounced as Goat-ham but a part of New York in the United States, whose inhabitants were likened to those in Nottinghamshire was spoken as Got-ham City. Its fame was in recent years extended by the caped crusader, Batman!

Places of Interest in the Neighbourhood
Contriving and Drawing All His Own Plans (Bunny)
A Serious Offence was Committed (Bradmore)
A Clergyman's Invention Lives On (Ruddington)

3 A Serious Offence was Committed

Position: Bradmore, 5 miles south of Nottingham
O.S. Map: Nottingham & Loughborough: Sheet No. 129: 1/50,000
Map Ref: SK 585/312
Access: Bradmore lies to the west of the A.60. Stafford House is at the corner of Farmer Street and Far Street.

Until 1860 church or ecclesiastical courts had considerable powers to deal with matters not now considered within the Church of England's jurisdiction. Canon law, which governed the working of these courts, was codified in the reign of James I on the principle that church and crown were in a state of friendly alliance for the punishment of wickedness and vice. The Canons relied on a system of church courts with the ultimate sanction of excommunication. Less serious offences could be dealt with by such punishments as serving penances or standing for a period in church in a white sheet.

Absence from church on the Sabbath was one such offence, but when it was compounded by 'prophaning', playing football, or as at Bradmore in 1618, morris dancing, it was even more serious. The plaque on Stafford House does not however state what punishment was meted out to Hugh Longley and his five companions.

Stafford House was formerly known as Barn Close and was one of a number of buildings designed by Sir Thomas Parkyns of the neighbouring village of Bunny (see No. 1). Another plaque on the building records that it dates from 1692 and was restored in 1989. It is now the European headquarters of an international group.

Places of Interest in the Neighbourhood
Contriving and Drawing All His Own Plans (Bunny)
The Men of Gotham – Foolish or Wise? (Gotham)
A Clergyman's Invention Lives On (Ruddington)

4 Some Corner of a Foreign Field

Position: Kinoulton, near Bingham
O.S. Map: Nottingham & Loughborough area: Sheet No. 129: 1/50,000
Map Ref: SK 678/314
Access: Kinoulton can be reached on a minor road on the east side of
the A.46 road, half a mile north of the junction with the A.606 road.
The track to Vimy Ridge Farm starts 300 yards north of the village.

The long line of poplar trees which starts just off the road between
Kinoulton and Owthorpe (see No. 6) is reminiscent of a scene in the
landscape of Belgium or Northern France. This is no accident, as the
poplars were planted as a reminder of the Flanders battlefields of the
1914-18 war. The lane which they border leads to a farm now called
Vimy Ridge Farm. Until 1919 this farm was known as Pasture Hill
Farm. Both the poplars and the name of the farm are to perpetuate the
memory of Lieut. Jesse Francis Montagu Hind who was killed in action
on 27th September 1916 during the battle of the Somme. There are said
to be 180 poplars lining the track, one for each of the officers killed in
the battle.

The poplars were planted by Jesse William Hind, who became Sir
Jesse in 1934, the father of Lieut. Hind. One of Sir Jesse's younger
brothers, Major Lawrence Arthur Hind, was also killed in action on the
1st July 1916. After Jesse Francis Montagu was killed his father purchased the farm at Kinoulton. Here he started a scheme for training 200
ex-servicemen in agriculture and finding work for them. Later, orphan
boys were also given a start in life there under a similar scheme.

Places of Interest in the Neighbourhood
A Roofless Ruin (Colston Bassett)
The Colonel's Devoted Lady (Owthorpe)
A Cavalier Stronghold (Wiverton)

The poplar-lined track to Vimy Ridge Farm, Kinoulton.

5 A Roofless Ruin

Position: Colston Bassett, near Bingham
O.S. Map: Nottingham & Loughborough area: Sheet No. 129: 1/50,000
Map Ref: SK 695/338
Access: The ruined church of St. Mary lies to the north-west of the village and is reached from a minor road leading north-east from the road to the village, two miles from the A.46 road opposite Cotgrave.

The church of St. Mary in its prime had traces of successive additions from Norman times onwards. It had two aisles and a south transept. But Colston Bassett is on the higher ground in the south-east of the county, known as the Wolds. In medieval times prosperity came from

The ruined church of St. Mary at Colston Bassett.

the wool of sheep which grazed on the hills. The decline of the wool trade, due to competition from elsewhere, led to a reduction in the population in the area. Some villages in the area ceased to exist and can be seen to-day only as irregular shapes in the fields showing where the buildings had been.

Colston Bassett did survive, but its church could no longer afford two aisles and the north one was demolished in the eighteenth century – consequently the new windows which had to be inserted reflect the style of the period. In the meantime more scientific principles of agriculture had been evolved and Colston Bassett's population increased. New houses were built a quarter of a mile down hill from the old church, near the River Smite. By the 1830's the village was prosperous enough to erect the handsome cross to commemorate the coronation of William IV. The population of the parish in the nineteenth century increased to 403 by 1841.

From 1877 the parish had had a new lord of the manor, Robert Millington Knowles who purchased the Hall and estate and became High Sheriff of Nottinghamshire in 1885. He was one of the original members of Nottinghamshire County Council when it was formed in 1889. His first wife died in 1873 and in 1890 his elder son John was drowned whilst salmon fishing, aged 21. It was about this time that the question of what should be done about the state of disrepair of St. Mary's Church was considered. It was decided to have a new church and Mr. Knowles met the cost, the new church St. John the Divine being dedicated to the memory of his son.

The old church was not demolished but the ecclesiastical authorities required that the roof be removed so that the building could not be used for some secular purpose. In 1898 Mr. T. M. Blagg visited the ruin which he described: "The church is roofless. Heaps of debris lie within the walls. Hemlock and elder grow in nave and aisle, thistles and nettles in the chancel. In the south transept a rabbit sprang from under my feet and sought refuge in a heap of stones and rubbish in the nave. The dead body of a half-fledged magpie lay on the ground alongside the bell-hammers and the Royal Arms, the canvas of the latter torn to shreds".

Places of Interest in the Neighbourhood
Some Corner of a Foreign Field (Kinoulton)
The Colonel's Devoted Lady (Owthorpe)
A Cavalier Stronghold (Wiverton)

6 The Colonel's Devoted Lady

Position: Owthorpe, near Bingham
O.S. Map: Nottingham & Loughborough area: Sheet No. 129: 1/50,000
Map Ref: SK 672/334
Access: Owthorpe is one mile on the west side of the A.46 road, four miles south of its junction with the A.52 road.

The tiny village of Owthorpe is a peaceful place, on a minor road. In fact it is probably quieter and less populated than it was in the seventeenth century. Like its near neighbour Colston Bassett (see No. 5) it is a wolds village which suffered depopulation. Some evidence of its earlier prosperity is the bracket at the west end of the church with two angels holding a shield. The church itself stands rather oddly on its own surrounded by fields.

Not only is the present church smaller than the earlier one, but another departure from the village's earlier status is the loss of its manor house. It was re-built about 1650 by Colonel John Hutchinson, to whom there is a monument in the church. The Hutchinson family had lived in the village since the sixteenth century and Sir Thomas and his two sons, John and George played a prominent part, on the side of the Roundheads or Parliamentarians, during the Civil War. John Hutchinson was the Governor of Nottingham Castle, and his wife Lucy later wrote *Memoirs of the Life of Colonel Hutchinson* which describes graphically the events of the war in Nottinghamshire. Her views are not always regarded as reliable, especially when she is defending her husband.

When the war ended, Colonel Hutchinson was one of those who signed the execution warrant of King Charles I. During the Commonwealth period he played little part in the government as he disagreed with Oliver Cromwell's policies in some respects. It was probably because of this that, at the restoration of the monarchy, he was not hanged as a regicide, as others were. However he was later arrested on ungrounded suspicion that he was involved in a plot to usurp the King and died a prisoner in Sandwich Castle in 1664.

Places of Interest in the Neighbourhood
Some Corner of a Foreign Field (Kinoulton)
A Roofless Ruin (Colston Bassett)
A Cavalier Stronghold (Wiverton)

7 A Clergyman's Invention Lives On

Position: Ruddington, 4 miles south of Nottingham
O.S. Map: Nottingham & Loughborough area: Sheet No. 129: 1/50,000
Map Ref: SK 572/328
Access: Ruddington Framework Knitting Museum is on Chapel Street.

Industrial history, like other branches, abounds in romantic stories.
James Watt is said to have foreseen the possibilities of steam power
from seeing boiling water pushing up the lid of a kettle whilst Samuel
Crompton's idea of a spinning mule is supposed to have been the result
of accidentally knocking over a spinning wheel. The stocking-frame, the
ancestor of much textile machinery, is the subject of an even more
romantic story. The Reverend William Lee, the curate at Calverton in
Nottinghamshire, was enamoured of a certain young lady who could
not spare time to respond to his overtures as she was too busy knitting
stockings by hand. To remove this obstacle he set to and produced a

William Lee's stocking frame.

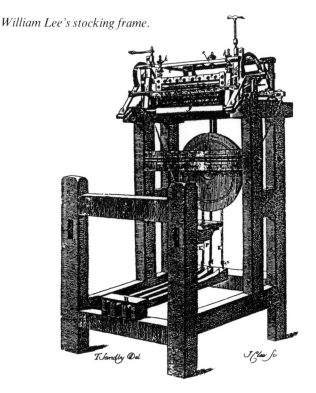

machine which would produce stockings much faster, leaving his intended more leisure time.

William Lee was a Nottingham man, born at or near Calverton and we know that he played a considerable part in the development of framework knitting from 1589. His early efforts to encourage the invention in England were frowned upon by Queen Elizabeth I, who feared the redundancy it would cause amongst hand knitters. As a result Lee took the invention to France but after his death the industry returned to England and slowly prospered.

Economic conditions in the late seventeenth century encouraged the spread of the industry in north-west Leicestershire and around the Nottinghamshire/Derbyshire border. It was a capital intensive industry, requiring money to buy the stocking frame and yarn, and was often concentrated in the hands of master hosiers who employed people to work stocking frames in their own homes.

By the end of the eighteenth century the frame work knitting industry had expanded considerably in the East Midlands and garments other than stockings were made. This led to some villages, including Ruddington, becoming more industrial than agricultural with production taking place in small workshops rather than in homes. It is appropriate therefore that the splendid collection of stocking frames should find its home in two of these workshops, with their distinctive windows.

The complex at Ruddington, administered by a Preservation Trust, also includes a small museum illustrating the history of the industry and houses typical of the worker's living quarters. Perhaps even more important, the Trust has arranged for the skill of operating the machines to be carried on and demonstrated.

Places of Interest in the Neighbourhood
Contriving and Drawing All His Own Plans (Bunny)
The Men of Gotham – Foolish or Wise? (Gotham)
A Serious Offence was Committed (Bradmore)

8 A Cavalier Stronghold

Position: Wiverton, near Bingham
O.S. Map: Nottingham & Loughborough area: Sheet No. 129: 1/50,000
Map Ref: SK 713/363
Access: Wiverton Hall is two miles south of Bingham, on a minor road commencing on the A.52 road, one mile east of the junction with the A.46 road.

There has been no village of Wiverton for hundreds of years, for Dr. Robert Thoroton writing in 1676 said it had completely disappeared. Visitors looking for it would have been equally unsuccessful if they had asked the way to it, unless they knew that the name was pronounced Werton. Wiverton Hall still survives and although it resembles the building which Dr. Thoroton illustrated, it was rebuilt in a similar style in 1814. The new house was built on to a fifteenth century gatehouse, part of the original mansion of the Chaworth family.

In 1890 Mrs. Chaworth Musters published a work of fiction entitled *A Cavalier Stronghold.* This tells of the part played in the Civil War by Wiverton Hall. Although a fictional account, it is based on the facts of the War, using the actual names of the participants. Prince Rupert stayed at Wiverton shortly before the defeat of the Royalists in 1645 and later Oliver Cromwell ordered the Hall, apart from the gateway, to be demolished.

Places of Interest in the Neighbourhood
Some Corner of a Foreign Field (Kinoulton)
A Roofless Ruin (Colston Bassett)
The Colonel's Devoted Lady (Owthorpe)

9 A Person of Very Weak and Slender Capacity

Position: Tollerton, near Nottingham
O.S. Map: Nottingham & Loughborough area: Sheet No. 129: 1/50,000
Map Ref: SK 616/352
Access: The village of Tollerton lies to the north of the A.606 road, along a minor road a mile east from the roundabout on the A.52 road.

The eccentricity of the design of the archway, one of the entrances to Tollerton Hall, is matched by the eccentricity of the man responsible for it. He was Pendock Barry, a member of a family which had owned the estate for centuries.

His life and character are well documented because when he died in 1833 he left a will in which he bequeathed the estate, not to his son Pendock Barry Neale (who later changed his name to Pendock Barry

Pendock Barry's gate-house at Tollerton.

Barry) but to James Butlin. The son immediately contested the will and the action went before the Judicial Committee of the Privy Council. The proceedings occupy 718 large pages of print and give a wealth of detail about life at Tollerton.

Pendock Barry Barry in his statement contesting the validity of his father's will claimed that he had been throughout all his life a person of very weak and slender capacity. He had been educated partly at Harrow and later at Oxford University which he left without a degree. Whilst at Oxford he was said to have acquired a taste for drink. When he married his wife managed his affairs until her death in 1811, instructing the servants not to contradict her husband and to keep a strict watch over him to prevent him doing mischief to himself and others.

Details were also given of what were described as frivolous and childish amusements. These included sitting on the box of a carriage, without horses, whip in hand and pretending to drive, and putting a saddle on one of his unfortunate servants and mounting him, booted and spurred. A regular duty of the servants was to go round picking up his clothes, which he used to throw out of his bedroom window.

Places of Interest in the Neighbourhood
A House with a Four-Fold View (Wilford)
Help for the Horse Rider (West Bridgford)
A Tall Servant (Clifton)

10 A Mathematical Genius

Position: Belvoir Hill, Nottingham
O.S. Map: Nottingham & Loughborough area: Sheet No. 129: 1/50,000
Map Ref: SK 585/397
Access: Green's Mill is on Belvoir Hill, just under a mile east of the city centre, at the top of Sneinton Road.

It is unusual in Britain to-day to see a windmill with a full set of sails moving with the wind. It is even more unusual to see such a sight in under a mile from a city centre. Sneinton Mill, often referred to as George Green's mill can be seen from a number of vantage points in and around the city. It was restored to its present state in 1986 since when it has been possible to buy flour ground by the mill. Yet is it probable that the mill would not have been restored at all had it not been the home of the remarkable George Green.

The hilly nature of the town of Nottingham meant that it was ringed round with windmills, most of which disappeared in the nineteenth century. Belvoir Hill at Sneinton was an ideal place for a windmill, the name denoting that it was possible to see Belvoir Castle, 15 miles away. The brick mill was erected there about 1807 by George Green senior who had a baker's business in Nottingham. About 1817 he moved from Nottingham to Belvoir Hill having had a house built adjoining the mill.

George's son, also George, had been born in Nottingham in 1793. His formal schooling at Goodacre's Academy only lasted a year, when he was aged 8, and he left to start work in his father's bakery. He moved with his parents to the Sneinton Mill and as his father grew older took over much of the milling work. In 1823 he joined Nottingham Subscription Library where he would have met some of Nottingham's leading intellectuals including those with an interest in science. It is however something of a mystery as to how Green was able to publish in 1828 as essay entitled "On the application of mathematical analysis to the theories of electricity and magnetism". In 1829 after his father died George junior inherited the mill and became reasonably wealthy. When he was aged 40, in 1833 he entered Gonville and Caius College, Cambridge, having for a number of years been encouraged in his mathematical studies by Sir Edward Ffrench Bromhead who was a member of a circle which included Charles Babbage, inventor of a calculating machine which led to computers, and John Herschell, a distinguished astronomer.

Green became an M.A. in 1839 and between 1833 and 1839 wrote 9

papers on various mathematical and scientific subjects. He returned to live at Sneinton where he died aged 47 in 1841. Although he was acknowledged as a gifted mathematician in his own lifetime, the full value and implications of his researches were not realised until over a hundred years after his death, when their importance to nuclear physics was realised.

Sneinton Mill, George Green's home, ceased to be used as a windmill in the 1860's and became rather derelict. It was later let to a floor polish manufacturer and in 1947 it caught fire. It remained as a ruin until a number of enthusiastic individuals, together with interested societies and local authorities started to restore the mill. It was officially opened as a restored mill, together with landscaped gardens and a car park in 1986. Adjoining the mill is a small Science Museum where models demonstrate some of the applications of George Green's work.

Places of Interest in the Neighbourhood
A Soldier of the Lord (Sneinton)
Tranquil in Zion (Nottingham)
A Gothic Joke (Nottingham)
Lighten our Darkness (Nottingham)

William Booth's statue outside his birthplace, Notintone Place, Sneinton.

11 A Soldier of The Lord

Position: Sneinton, Nottingham
O.S. Map: Nottingham & Loughborough area: Sheet 129: 1/50,000
Map Ref: SK 588/397
Access: Notintone Place is on Sneinton Road, opposite St. Stephen's
Church, a quarter of a mile from Carlton Road, A.612.

At one time Notintone Place, Sneinton, had houses on each side.
Today, only three of them remain and have been incorporated into a
new development for the Salvation Army. One of the three houses, No.
12, is now a museum and was the birthplace in 1829 of William Booth.
At the age of 13 he became apprenticed to a pawnbroker in Nottingham, working without wages for six years. He attended the Wesleyan
Chapel in Broad Street and when he was 17 he was inspired by an
American evangelist to carry out similar work. He left Nottingham
when his apprenticeship was finished and went to live in London where
he became a Methodist minister. In 1861 he resigned as a minister and
began to travel around holding revivalist meetings. Four years later he
started mission work in the East End of London which led to the
development of the Salvation Army. The movement with its emphasis
on social work among the less fortunate as well as religious observance
spread throughout England, and later to many other parts of the world.

   The early years of the movement owed much to the dynamic inspira-
tion of William Booth and the statue of him outside his birthplace
typifies his fighting spirit which was characterised by adopting military
ranks for Salvation Army officers. As General William Booth he was
honoured by his native city by being made an honorary freeman in
1905.

Places of Interest in the Neighbourhood
A Mathematical Genius (Sneinton)
Tranquil in Zion (Nottingham)
A Gothic Joke (Nottingham)
Lighten our Darkness (Nottingham)

12 Tranquil in Zion

Position: Nottingham
O.S. Map: Nottingham & Loughborough area: Sheet No. 129: 1/50,000
Map Ref: SK 578/403
Access: The entrance to St. Mary's Rest Garden is at the junction of
Bath Street and St. Ann's Well Road.

Now a restful oasis although less than half a mile from Nottingham's
busy city centre, the Rest Garden was used as a cemetery from 1835
until the early years of this century. Some of the headstones can still
be seen around the boundary walls but there are only a few monu-
ments still in their original positions. One of these, in the south-west
corner, is in the form of a recumbent lion. The inscription tells us that it
marks the burial place of William Thompson, better known as Bendigo.
He was born in Nottingham in 1811, one of a large family and became famous for his exploits as a bare-knuckle pugilist. By defeating a
number of well known fighters in the 1830's he became the champion
of England. Unfortunately he was unable to control his temper particularly when under the influence of alcohol and served twenty eight
prison sentences, mainly for drunkenness and assault.

   Eventually he was converted to religion by Richard Weaver, a
revivalist preacher and spent his later years touring the country and
addressing popular religious meetings. He achieved the status of a
sporting hero and when he died near Nottingham in 1880 a crowd of
20,000 watched the funeral procession and the burial service in St.
Mary's cemetery. In 1891 a number of his admirers subscribed to the
cost of the memorial to him in the cemetery.

Places of Interest in the Neighbourhood
A Mathematical Genius (Sneinton)
A Soldier of the Lord (Sneinton)
A Gothic Joke (Nottingham)
Lighten our Darkness (Nottingham)

13 A Gothic Joke

Position: Nottingham
O.S. Map: Nottingham & Loughborough area: Sheet No. 129: 1/50,000
Map Ref: SK 575/400
Access: George Street is on the south side of Parliament Street and
north of Carlton Street.

Within a quarter of a mile of Nottingham's Old Market Square there
are eight distinctive buildings all designed by the same architect. Some
he signed, either as Fothergill Watson, or Watson Fothergill. The two
names were used deliberately, for a reason perhaps indicative of the
arthitect's personality and the unique character of his designs. He was
born Fothergill Watson on 12th July 1841 at Mansfield, the son of
Robert Watson and his second wife, formerly Mary Ann Fothergill. His
christian name was thus his mother's maiden name. In 1892 he changed

Watson Fothergill's office in George Street, Nottingham.

his name by deed poll by transposing his two names, so ensuring the perpetuation of his mother's line in an attempt to trace his ancestry back to William the Conqueror.

Watson Fothergill lived to the age of 87 and many anecdotes of his character and eccentricities have been recorded, some of which have no doubt improved in the telling. Some of his so-called eccentricity probably arose from his refusal to abandon habits of an earlier and much different age. He lived long enough to see the motor-car coming into more general use, but he was used to driving to his office in a carriage with a liveried coachman and footman. In his later years his silk hat would set him apart from those in bowlers and cloth caps. A strict and formal man, who when on visits to a building site would only address workmen through a third person, he nevertheless had a strong sense of humour.

It is this sense of humour which has led architectural critics to refer to his own office, No. 15 George Street, as a Gothic joke. He built it in 1895, after he had been practising as an architect in Nottingham for thirty years. By then he had already established a reputation as one of Nottingham's leading architects, having designed houses, banks, hotels and public buildings. Their individuality was marked by his use of polychrome bricks, often deep red and with contrasting bands of blue, and by decorative features such as turrets, oriel windows, barge boards and friezes. 15 George Street illustrates a number of these features and in addition is in some ways autobiographical. The central figure at first floor level is of a medieval architect with a Gothic cathedral at this feet. For Fothergill was a convinced Gothic revivalist who wrote 'Scott's best work was the St. Pancras Hotel'. He included on the frontage the names and dates of three Victorian architects, Scott, Burges and Shaw and busts of two others, including Pugin whom he regarded as his mentors. His supreme joke must have been the bust, in the building on George Street, of George (Edmund) Street.

Places of Interest in the Neighbourhood
A Mathematical Genius (Sneinton)
A Soldier of the Lord (Sneinton)
Tranquil in Zion (Nottingham)
Lighten our Darkness (Nottingham)

14 Lighten our Darkness

Position: Nottingham
O.S. Map: Nottingham & Loughborough area: Sheet No. 129 1/50,000
Map Ref: SK 577/397
Access: St. Mary's Church is on High Pavement with entrances to the
churchyard on Stoney Street and St. Mary's Gate as well.

Of the four entrances to St. Mary's churchyard two of them, the one at
the north-west corner and the other at the south-east, have wrought
iron brackets supporting a loop. These were erected in the eighteenth
century as early lamp posts. In the loops were placed buckets containing whale oil with a wick which was lighted.

The whale oil was stored in the cellar of the old Guildhall in Weekday
Cross, at the western end of High Pavement. Those living nearby would
not be too pleased with this arrangement, as the oil gave off an un-
pleasant odour, especially in summer. Dealers in whale oil used to dis-
play a whale's jaw bone outside their premises to indicate that they sold
it. One of these can be seen in Nottingham outside the 'Royal Children'
public house on Castle Gate.

The inhabitants of Nottingham seemed to have managed without
street lighting until the eighteenth century. It is first mentioned in 1705,
when the Common Council agreed to pay £2 to Samuel Smith for the
convex light which he had installed outside his house when he was
Mayor in 1703. The Council also decided that this light should be
placed outside the door of each successive Mayor in future.

Gas lighting was used first in Nottingham in 1819, causing alarm to
some of the townspeople as the gas was supplied to the lamps through
pipes laid in the streets. They thought that the pipes were red-hot and
they would burn their feet if they walked over them.

Places of Interest in the Neighbourhood
A Mathematical Genius (Sneinton)
A Soldier of the Lord (Sneinton)
Tranquil in Zion (Nottingham)
A Gothic Joke (Nottingham)

15 A House with a Four-Fold View

Position: Wilford, near Nottingham
O.S. Map: Nottingham & Loughborough area: Sheet No. 129: 1/50,000
Map Ref: SK 567/378
Access: Wilford Village can be approached on foot or cycle by a bridge over the River Trent, three-quarters of a mile south of the Midland Railway Station. Vehicles can enter the village (no through road) from the B.679 road, Wilford Lane.

The churchyard of St. Wilfrid's stands on a small cliff overlooking the River Trent. In the north-west corner of the churchyard stands a charming brick structure, a gazebo or summer-house. It has four windows and when first built there would be a more or less rural view from each of them. In those days, the town of Nottingham, a mile away, was separated by meadows. Today Wilford is part of the City of Nottingham and the view is rather different.

The summer-house was renovated a few years ago and a tablet on an inside wall tells us that it was used for a rather less pleasant function at times. The nearness of the River Trent meant that they were drowning accidents from time to time. Bodies recovered from the river near Wilford were placed in the basement of the summer-house until an inquest had been held, usually in the nearby Ferry Inn.

Places of Interest in the Neighbourhood
A Person of Very Weak and Slender Capacity (Tollerton)
Help for the Horse Rider (West Bridgford)
A Tall Servant (Clifton)

Gazebo in St. Wilfrid's church yard, Wilford.

16 Help for the Horse Rider

Position: West Bridgford, Nottingham
O.S. Map: Nottingham & Loughborough: Sheet No. 129: 1/50,000
Map Ref: SK 587/377
Access: West Bridgford Park is half-a-mile south of Trent Bridge, along
Bridgford Road.

A mounting-block for horse riders may now seem unnecessary in a
public park. The one in West Bridgford has been there for two hundred
years or so and if not a necessity then it was convenient, especially for
lady riders. Moreover it was not then a public park. It was part of the
parkland attached to The Hall, a red-brick mansion erected between
1768 and 1774 by Mundy Musters, who owned most of the land at West
Bridgford.

In 1776 John Musters married Sophia Heywood, a noted beauty who
was a lady of the bedchamber to the Queen and who would have
undoubtedly used the mounting-block. Mrs. Musters is depicted in a
painting by Stubbs riding on horseback with Colwick Hall in the
background.

Mounting block in the grounds of The Hall, West Bridgford.

Another visitor to The Hall was Mary Chaworth, wife of John and Sophia Musters' son, also John. She was known as 'Byron's Mary' (see No. 41). After the Vaughans left The Hall it was let to Lewis Heymann, a German who had settled in England and started a prosperous lace curtain manufacturer's business in Nottingham's Lace Market. His son Albert continued to live at The Hall until 1924, having purchased it outright. When he left, he sold The Hall and its grounds to West Bridgford Urban District Council. The Council used The Hall as its headquarters and made the grounds into a public park. In 1974 the functions of the Urban District Council were taken over by Rushcliffe Borough Council. Both Councils have fortunately been mindful enough of the mounting block's historical importance to retain it.

Places of Interest in the Neighbourhood
A Person of Very Weak and Slender Capacity (Tollerton)
A House with a Four-Fold View (Wilford)
A Tall Servant (Clifton)

17 A Tall Servant

Position: Clifton Village, near Nottingham
O.S. Map: Nottingham & Loughborough area: Sheet No. 129: 1/50,000
Map Ref: SK 541/348
Access: Clifton village is on the west side of the A.453 road, 3 ½ miles
south-west of Nottingham. The church, St. Mary's, is at the west end of
the village at the end of the main street.

Whilst we are sometimes able to find out the physical features of people
who lived in past centuries, such descriptions as have been recorded are
usually in general terms, such as 'tall' or 'stout'. It is rare that the exact
height of our ancestors is known. In the north porch of St. Mary's
Church, Clifton, there is a permanent record of one man's height. On
the arch of the porch are carved his initials 'I.P.' and another inscribed
mark shows that he was 6 feet 4 inches tall. The initials stand for the
name by which he was known in the village, Indian Prince.

In the south transept is a floor-stone which is inscribed:
> 'Here lieth interred the body of Joseph commonly called the Black Prince
> who was converted to the Christian Faith Anno Domini 1675 and died on
> the First day of June Anno Domini 1685 in hope of a better life'

Joseph must have been a most unusual sight to the villagers of seventeenth century Clifton, for not only was he tall but he was black. How
and why he came to be a servant to the lord of the manor of Clifton is
not recorded. The Clifton family take their name from the village, and
in 1608 Gervase Clifton, was created a baronet by King James I. Sir
Gervase, who lived to the age of 80 and had seven wives, was noted for
his hospitality and generosity. Doctor Robert Thoroton who wrote the
first history of Nottinghamshire, published in 1676, knew Sir Gervase
well. He refers to Sir Gervase's son, also Gervase, as 'the wretched
unfortunate Sir Gervase his Father's greatest Foil'. It is probable that it
was this Sir Gervase, the second baronet from 1666 when his father
died, who brought Joseph the Indian Prince to Clifton. The slave trade
was well established by the seventeenth century and Sir Gervase could
well have brought Joseph from the West Indies.

Places of Interest in the Neighbourhood
A Person of Very Weak and Slender Capacity (Tollerton)
A House with a Four-Fold View (Wilford)
Help for the Horse Rider (West Bridgford)

18 Early Horse Power

Position: Wollaton, Nottingham
O.S. Map: Nottingham & Loughborough area: Sheet No. 129: 1/50,000
Map Ref: SK 531/393
Access: There are several entrances to Wollaton Park, the nearest for
the Industrial Museum being on Wollaton Rd (Map ref. SK 529/398).
The Industrial Museum is 600 yards from here in the former stable
block adjoining the Hall.

The changing face of industry in Nottinghamshire is well documented
in the Industrial Museum, and the horse-gin there is a good example of
how mining methods have changed over the centuries. A deed of 1348
refers to the transfer of a half part of a mine of sea-coal at Cossall (see
No.30). Coal was referred to as sea-coal, because it was mainly found in
the north-east of England and transferred to its main market, London,

Horse gin in the Industrial Museum, Wollaton.

by sea.

As the deed shows there was also a source of supply at Cossall, part of an exposed coalfield on the Nottinghamshire and Derbyshire border. It was obtained from shallow mines known as bell-pits. A shaft was dug and the colliers dug out the coal until a bell-shaped cavity was formed, which was then abandoned as further working would cause it to collapse.

The coalfield sloped downwards from west to east and as supplies near the surface were used up it was necessary to sink deeper shafts which could not be reached by ladder. The idea evolved of lowering men down the shafts in large buckets. The invention of the horse-gin made the task much easier by transforming the circular horizontal motion of a horse towing a large beam, to which was attached a rope, to a vertical movement by means of a pulley. With the invention of the steam engine this method gradually became superseded. The one in the Industrial Museum was first used at Langton in 1844 and continued to be used occasionally for inspection at Pinxton until 1950.

It is appropriate that the horse-gin is in an Industrial Museum adjoining Wollaton Hall as Sir Francis Willoughby, who had it built in 1588, paid for the Ancaster stone from Lincolnshire, with which it was built, by coal. He had a mine at Wollaton and the coal from there was carried along what can justifiably claim to be the world's first railway. A track was laid down from Wollaton to the River Trent and the coal was carried along it in horse-drawn waggons.

Places of Interest in the Neighbourhood
A Twisted Stump of Rock (Bramcote)
A Moveable Cross (Stapleford)
A Relic of a Palladian House (Nuthall)
A Recusant's Retreat (Cossall)

19 A Twisted Stump of Rock

Position: Hemlock Stone, near Stapleford
O.S. Map: Nottingham & Loughborough area: Sheet No. 129: 1/50,000
Map Ref: SK 500/388
Access: The Hemlock Stone is on the west side of the A.6002 road
about 200 yards north of its junction with the A.6007 road.

"They had expected a venerable and dignified monument. They found a
little, gnarled, twisted stump of rock, something like a decayed mush-
room standing out pathetically on the side of a field." The monument
was the Hemlock Stone and 'they' were Paul Morel and a group of his
friends, whilst the description is from D.H. Lawrence's novel *Sons and
Lovers*, written in 1912. Lawrence's early novels have as their background the district around Eastwood where he lived for his first 21
years. In some cases the place names are disguised but in *Sons and
Lovers*, which clearly describes incidents from Lawrence's own life,
many are not. The central character Paul Morel, aged 19, had organised
a walk on a Good Friday and Lawrence writes, using the actual place
names, "In Ilkeston the colliers were waiting in gangs for the public
houses to open. It was a town of idleness and loafing. At Stanton Gate
the iron foundry blazed . . . At Trowell they crossed again from Derbyshire into Nottinghamsire. They came to the Hemlock Stone at
dinner-time. Its field was crowded with folk from Nottingham and
Ilkeston".

This 'twisted stump of rock' has been much written about elsewhere.
William Stukeley, an eighteenth century antiquarian visited it and
wrote 'A little beyond Wollaton Hall, in the road, upon the brow of the
hill, is a high rugged piece of rock, called Hemlock-stone, seen at a good
distance: probably it is the remains of a quarry dug from around it.' A
local writer in the nineteenth century, believed that the ancient waters
gave the Hemlock Stone much of its present appearance and that the
rains and winds of later periods greatly modified it. This is a more
rational explanation than one which appeared about the same time,
anonymously and in verse. This recounted how the devil, annoyed by a
monk at Lenton Abbey, hurled a large rock at the monk but missed his
target by several miles.

A rather more scientific explanation was given in 1966 in *Nottingham
and Its Region* by F.M. Taylor. He describes the stone as an interesting
erosion feature and states that the prominent capping offered greater
resistance to weathering because the sand of which the rock is com-

The Hemlock Stone at Bramcote.

posed is irregularly cemented by barium sulphate.

Places of Interest in the Neighbourhood
Early Horse Power (Wollaton)
A Moveable Cross (Stapleford)
A Relic of a Palladian House (Nuthall)
A Recusant's Retreat (Cossall)

20 A Moveable Cross

Position: Stapleford, near Nottingham
O.S. Map: Nottingham & Loughborough: Sheet No. 129: 1/50,000
Map Ref: SK 489/373
Access: The church of St. Helen is on the B.6003 road, one mile north of the junction with the A.52 road.

Stapleford is a mainly industrial area which started to grow from a small village a hundred years ago. Although its church has thirteenth and fourteenth century parts, the churchyard contains an even earlier monument. This is the Anglo-Saxon cross, described as the most important pre-Conquest monument in the county. The original shaft is 10 feet high and the base and top were renewed in 1820. The cross is decorated with typical Anglo-Saxon interlacings, with one face having a doll-like figure at the top.

Perhaps equally remarkable is that the cross has survived being moved twice. Until the eighteenth century it stood in the church-yard but was then moved to the street outside. It stood there until 1928 when it was not only becoming something of a hazard to traffic but was itself in danger of being damaged.

Places of Interest in the Neighbourhood
Early Horse Power (Wollaton)
A Twisted Stump of Rock (Bramcote)
A Relic of a Palladian House (Nuthall)
A Recusant's Retreat (Cossall)

Saxon cross at Stapleford.

21 A Little Old Lady Remembered

Position: Bingham
O.S. Map: Nottingham & Loughborough area: Sheet No. 129: 1/50,000
Map Ref: SK 707/400
Access: The church of All Saints lies to the east of the market place.
Bingham is now by-passed by the A.52 road.

In 1928 Southwell Diocese allowed the Church of All Saints, Bingham,
to place an oak figure on the south pillar of the chancel arch as a
memorial to Ann Harrison, born 20th September 1829 and died 14th
January 1928, together with the words 'All her long life a constant
worshipper here'. The oak figure, 18 inches high, shows her dressed in
bonnet and shawl, with a stick in one hand and a large fish basket in the
other. Ann Harrison was as generous as she was humble. During the
First World War a weekly collection was taken in the church to provide
a roll of honour of those killed in the war. About this time, old age
pensions were increased from 5/- per week to 7/6d. As half-crowns
began to appear in the collection plate, someone gently suggested to
Ann Harrison that 3d. or 6d. would be quite sufficient. Ann Harrison
promptly told her to mind her own business!

In fact the half-crowns came from a small business venture. Using the
fish-basket depicted in the church, she went round Bingham to friends
and acquaintances collecting potato peelings and other refuse. These
she sold for 5/- per week to a small-holder for fattening pigs. During her
lifetime she steadfastly refused to have her photograph put in the book
containing the roll of honour. After her death this was done. Another
memento of her in the church is her old armchair.

Ann Harrison was the daughter of an agricultural labourer, and when
her mother died she looked after her father until he died. She never
married.

Places of Interest in the Neighbourhood
A Martyr's Seat (Aslockton)
A Pile of Old Shoes (Scarrington)

Ann Harrison's statue in the Church of All Saints, Bingham.

22 A Martyr's Seat

Position: Aslockton, 3 miles east of Bingham
O.S. Map: Nottingham & Loughborough area: Sheet No. 129: 1/50,000
Map Ref: SK 743/401
Access: Aslockton lies about three-quarters of a mile north of the A.52
road, 4 miles east of its junction with the A.46.

Cranmer's Mound was not so named because it was built by Thomas
Cranmer. The future Archbishop was born at Aslockton in 1489 and
received his first education in the village school so it is highly probable
that he climbed on the mound, which was old when he was born. It is in
fact a well preserved motte, sixteen feet high, probably dating back to
the 12th or 13th centuries. Mottes were usually built to form the base of
a castle, but there is no evidence here of such a structure. To the south-
east of the mound can be seen two rectangular platforms surrounded by
broad ditches which could well have been the site of the Cranmer's
house. If so, young Thomas would almost certainly have known the
mound on which he is said to have sat and gazed at the surrounding
countryside.

   After becoming Archdeacon of Taunton he by chance was involved in
the efforts of King Henry VIII to divorce his wife Catherine of Aragon.
As a result Henry made him Archbishop of Canterbury in 1533. It
was of course Henry's struggles with the Pope which was to lead
to the break with Rome and the English Reformation. Cranmer as
Archbishop played a major role in the establishment of protestantism
as the English religion, which was later to prove his undoing. After
Henry VIII's death and the short reign of Edward VI, Henry's daughter
Mary became queen. She had retained the Roman Catholic religion and
when Cranmer, together with Nicholas Ridley and Hugh Latimer,
refused to abandon their beliefs they were tried as heretics and in 1554,
burnt at the stake, becoming known as the English Martyrs.

   Cranmer's father's memorial in Whatton church bears the family
arms of three cranes. Henry VIII changed this to three pelicans, telling
Cranmer prophetically that he should, like the pelican, be prepared to
shed his blood for his beliefs. 'You are liked to be tested at length if you
stand to your tackling'.

Places of Interest in the Neighbourhood
A Little Old Lady Remembered (Bingham)
A Pile of Old Shoes (Scarrington)

23 A Pile of Old Shoes

Position: Scarrington, near Bingham
O.S. Map: Nottingham & Loughborough area: Sheet No. 129: 1/50,000
Map Ref: SK 735/415
Access: Scarrington lies one and a half miles north of the A.52 road, on
a minor road starting a mile east of Bingham.

George Flinders was the blacksmith at Scarrington Forge for 51 years.
In 1945 he started to build a conical stack of used horseshoes outside
the Forge. Initially, the large shoes at the bottom came from the dying
race of farm horses. They grow smaller towards the top with shining
featherweight plates of duralumin taken from racehorses trained in the
district.
    When Mr. Flinders retired in April 1965 the stack had grown to 17
feet, comprising some 50,000 shoes. The toes of the shoes were pointed
outwards and the nails were left in, so that the shoes interlocked. The

Pile of horse-shoes at Scarrington.

stack was estimated to weigh 10 tons and measured 19 feet 6 inches in circumference at the base.

In 1973 the stack was sold to a businessman who proposed selling individual shoes to Americans as a souvenir of 'Olde England'. After five hundred shoes had been removed protests from the local inhabitants led to Nottinghamshire County Council buying the stack to preserve it and keep it in place. There is an information board near the stack, giving its history as well as that of the nearby pinfold where stray animals were impounded. The board proclaims that it is the 'largest known stack of horseshoes in the world'.

A similar stack is now being built in the nearby village of Aslockton, whilst a village near Malton in Yorkshire has a farm yard with two similar stacks either side of the gate.

Places of Interest in the Neighbourhood
A Little Old Lady Remembered (Bingham)
A Martyr's Seat (Aslockton)

Sibthorpe dovecote.

24 The Birds Have Flown

Position: Sibthorpe, 7 miles south of Newark
O.S. Map: Nottingham & Loughborough: Sheet No. 129: 1/50,000
Map Ref: SK 765/454
Access: On the east side of the A.46 through Flintham to the village of Sibthorpe a distance of 2 ½ miles. The dovecote is in a field about 200 yards east of the church.

Dovecotes or pigeon houses were in use by the Romans, but their existence in England is not recorded until the middle ages. Pigeons were kept as an alternative source of food, being particularly valuable in the winter months when fresh meat was scarce. As well as providing food, the pigeon dung was used as manure, for medicinal purposes and in the manufacture of saltpetre for gun-powder.

Dovecotes existed in a number of different styles, some free-standing, others part of farm buildings. In 1927 J. Whitaker published *The Medieval Dovecotes of Nottinghamshire.* He listed 31, all of which he had visited, but in fact 6 of them were outside the county and he restricted his list to free-standing structures. He described the Sibthorpe cote as the largest and most striking in Nottinghamshire. "The most unobservant must be struck by this great circular pigeon cote", he added. He measured the cote which stood 60 feet to the weather vane, was ninety-eight feet round at a height of four feet, with walls three feet thick. He also counted the nesting places which were in twenty-eight rows of forty five, 1,260 in all.

Sibthorpe had a collegiate church in medieval times and the dovecote belonged to it. It was probably built in the 12th or 13th century. There is documentary evidence of the dovecote from 1601 when it was mentioned in a deed of sale of the manor house.

A more recent work *Dovecotes of Nottinghamshire* by John Severn, published in 1986 gives information on 129 surviving dovecotes of all types in the county, but this number excludes two districts where they had not yet been recorded.

Places of Interest in the Neighbourhood
One Huge Folly (Elston)
7004 Killed in Battle (East Stoke)

25 Holder of the Purse Strings

Position: Lambley, near Nottingham
O.S. Map: Nottingham & Loughborough area: Sheet No. 129: 1/50,000
Map Ref: SK 631/454
Access: Lambley, 5 miles north-east of Nottingham, can be reached by
a minor road from the B.684 road, about 2 miles east of it.

Holy Trinity church at Lambley is a fine example of perpendicular architecture, a rarity amongst Nottinghamshire villages. The east end has
a five light window and flanking it outside are two carved panels each
depicting a purse. This was the badge of Ralph Cromwell who became
Lord Treasurer of England in 1433. His father, also Ralph, was the first
Baron Cromwell. He died in 1398 and there is a monument to him in the
church.

His son Ralph was born at the old Manor House at Lambley. As a
young man he served as a soldier under Henry V at the Battle of Agin-
court. At the age of 26 he was appointed as Governor to the King and
Queen of France. When Henry VI became King, Cromwell was one of
seventeen members of a council appointed to run the nation during the
King's minority.

The post of Lord Treasurer was a lucrative one, but one not without
its dangers in an age when political differences were often settled by
violence – indeed he survived an attempt to murder him in 1449. He
continued to prosper and spent much of his wealth on buildings.

Places of Interest in the Neighbourhood
Fashion Made Him an Idol (Arnold)
An Orange Seller's Estate (Bestwood)

Ralph Cromwell's badge at Lambley.

48

26 Fashion Made Him an Idol

Position: Arnold, 4 miles north of Nottingham
O.S. Map: Nottingham & Loughborough area: Sheet No. 129: 1/50,000
Map Ref: SK 585/456
Access: High Street can be reached from the A.60 road either by
Nottingham Road from the south or by Cross Street from the north.

Arnold became an industrialised village in the nineteenth century as a
result of the expansion of the hosiery trade. A history of the town
published in 1913 had a chapter headed 'Worthies and Notables' which
only included a small number of names. None of them, with one exception, ever achieved lasting fame, even locally. The exception, Richard
Parkes Bonington who died aged 26, is known not only in this country
but abroad. He received the signal honour of an entry in the *Dictionary
of National Biography,* for the quantity and quality of his drawings
and paintings in oils and watercolours. He lived in France from the
age of fifteen and many of his watercolours are of coastal and marine
scenes in a style influenced by one of England's finest artists, J.W.M.
Turner, whom Bonington revered. After his early death, his works became eagerly sought after in France, leading the *Morning Post* to com-
ment that 'fashion made him an idol'. The 4th Marquess of Hertford, a
man who knew what he liked in art, acquired many of Bonington's
works. This was fortunate for England, as the daughter-in-law of the
Marquess, Lady Wallace, eventually bequeathed his collection to what
became the Wallace Collection.

England did not in fact appreciate Bonington's art in the nineteenth
century to the extent that France did. Eventually however he did receive
local recognition and a statue of him was erected in the forecourt of
Nottingham's School (later College) of Art, thanks to a local architect,
Watson Fothergill (see No. 13).

Arnold, where he was born, somewhat belatedly commemorated the
fact by a plaque affixed to the house where he was born, No. 79
High Street. The plaque had been designed by Joseph Else, the principal of the Nottingham School of Art, and was unveiled on October
1929 by Robert Mellors, an Arnold man who wrote extensively on
Nottinghamshire history.

Places of Interest in the Neighbourhood
Holder of the Purse Strings (Lambley)
An Orange Seller's Estate (Bestwood)

27 An Orange Seller's Estate

Position: Bestwood Country Park
O.S. Map: Nottingham & Loughborough: Sheet No. 129: 1/50,000
Map Ref: SK 569/465
Access: From the A.60 road, 3½ miles north of Nottingham, take the
B.6004 road on the west side. After 300 yards turn right along Queens
Bower Road, then right again after a further 300 yards along Bestwood
Lodge Drive. Bestwood Lodge Hotel and Bestwood Country Park are
just under one mile along this road.

Time has turned full circle at Bestwood. In 1364 Edward III issued
letters patent from his park at Bestwood. Today it is again a park, but a
country park which can be enjoyed by all. It was once a royal park, part
of the royal forest of Sherwood, until the Tudors, ever needing money
for the royal coffers leased it to Sir John Byron. Later, it was similarly
granted to various tenants including the Earl of Rutland, and in the
reign of Charles II to Lord Willoughby of Parham. In 1681 however
parts of the park were leased to farmers by Nell Gwynne. She had given
birth to two sons, in 1670 and 1671, both fathered by Charles II. Just
before he died he is said to have declared 'Let not poor Nelly starve'.

Bestwood Park was therefore to provide for her until her death in
1687, when she left it to her elder son, Charles Beauclerk, who had been
created Duke of St. Albans in 1684. The estate remained in the St.
Albans family until about fifty years ago.

The 10th Duke of St. Albans had a new Lodge built in the 1860's,
designed by S.S. Teulon in a style reminiscent of fourteenth century
architecture. It is now a hotel and nearby stands a cross. At the base of
the cross are plaques which tell at some length the history of the parish.
Until 1877 it was a detached part of the parish of Lenton, some five
miles away. In that year Lenton was incorporated into the borough of
Nottingham and a new parish of Bestwood St. Albans created.

Places of Interest in the Neighbourhood
Holder of the Purse Strings (Lambley)
Fashion Made Him an Idol (Arnold)

50

28 The Rod Not Spared

Position: Bulwell, Nottingham
O.S. Map: Nottingham & Loughborough area: Sheet No. 129: 1/50,000
Map Ref: SK 539/452
Access: The Old Grammar School is in Strelley Street in Bulwell, 4 miles north of Nottingham. Strelley Street is at the end of the pedestrianised Commercial Road from the Market Place.

In 1667 George Strelley of Hempshill drew up a deed by which he provided a Free School 'for the educating and teaching young children of the Inhabitants of the Parish of Bulwell'. The number of children was limited to thirty and the founder endowed the school with an income to pay the salary of a teacher and to maintain the building. He stated that the catechism was to be taught, a chapter of the Bible was to be read daily and the children were to be taught Latin. In addition they were to be taught "to write and read written hand and to cypher and cast accounts".

The population of Bulwell in 1667 would be about 250 people, in about 50 families. Most of the men would be engaged in agriculture or quarrying, as Bulwell was noted for its excellent stone. There would have been little formal education for children at that time and the Free School played an important part in the life of the town until its closure in 1867.

In 1929 an historical pageant called 'A Dream of Bulwell', in twelve episodes, was presented at the Olympia Theatre. One was 'The Strelley School' and the programme contained the following poetic introduction:

> The house is standing to this day,
> Where Joseph Calladine held sway,
> And ruled with rod his scholar band,
> One of the earliest in the land.
> He read the Bible day by day,
> And taught his boys to work and play,
> Reading, writing, arithmetic,
> Impressed by whackings from his stick.

Places of Interest in the Neighbourhood
A Victorian Iron Monument (Bennerley)
Bad, Mad and Dangerous to Know (Hucknall)
From Whence the Phoenix Rose (Eastwood)

29 A Relic of a Palladian House

Position: Nuthall, 4 miles north west of Nottingham
O.S. Map: Nottingham & Loughborough area: Sheet No. 129: 1/50,000
Map Ref: SK 515/445
Access: The Three Ponds public house is on the B.600 road opposite St. Patrick's Church.

The large stone gate pier at the entrance to the car park of the modern public house at Nuthall now seems redundant. But it has stood there for nearly two hundred and fifty years, and is the only reminder of Nuthall Temple – demolished in 1929.

Nuthall Temple was built in 1754-57 as a Palladian villa for Sir Charles Sedley. Its architect was Thomas Wright, who was also an astronomer and landscape gardener. The house was square with a large dome in the centre and was surrounded by parkland with lawns, gardens and a lake. Most of the grounds now lie beneath the M1 motorway.

Places of Interest in the Neighbourhood
Early Horse Power (Wollaton)
A Twisted Stump of Rock (Bramcote)
A Moveable Cross (Stapleford)
A Recusant's Retreat (Cossall)

Gate pier, relic of Nuthall Temple.

30 A Recusant's Retreat

Position: Cossall, 5 miles west of Nottingham
O.S. Map: Nottingham & Loughborough area: Sheet No. 129: 1/50,000
Map Ref: SK 484/423
Access: About a mile and a half south from the A.610, along the A.6096
on the east side is a road signposted to Cossall.

The Willoughby Almshouses at Cossall were erected in 1685 and were
endowed by George Willoughby. They were for four men who were
given 5/- (25p) per week and four women who had to make do with 4/-
(20p) per week. All also had a yearly allowance of coals and a suit of
clothes every two years.

George Willoughby was a member of the family which took its name
from the south Nottinghamshire village. They purchased and acquired
through marriages considerable lands in Nottinghamshire, including
Wollaton where probably the most remarkable Willoughby, Sir Francis, built the Hall in 1588. Some branches of the family, including that
at Cossall, adhered to the old Catholic religion but were not allowed to
worship openly. In 1746 the Rector of Cossall stated there was a room
in the almshouses where occasionally a Popish Priest held services in
great secrecy attended only by a few of the almspeople.

A curious feature of the almshouses is the double wall at the front,
which seems to have the same function as barriers outside school
entrances. However, one can hardly imagine it was necessary to stop the
tenants rushing out into the road in 1685, when the only traffic was an
occasional horse and cart.

D.H. Lawrence knew Cossall well and used it, as he did much of the
surrounding area, as the background to some of his novels. In *The
White Peacock* he writes of 'the shadow from the sun-dial on the warm
old almshouses' whilst in *The Rainbow* much of the action takes place in
Cossethay, which is clearly identifiable as Cossall. A few yards from the
almshouses at Church Cottage is a wall plaque describing its part in the
novel.

Places of Interest in the Neighbourhood
Early Horse Power (Wollaton)
A Twisted Lump of Rock (Bramcote)
A Moveable Cross (Stapleford)
A Relic of a Palladian House (Nuthall)

31 A Victorian Iron Monument

Position: Bennerley Viaduct, near Kimberley
O.S. Map: Nottingham & Loughborough area: Sheet No. 129: 1/50,000
Map Ref: SK 475/440
Access: The Viaduct is now sealed off but can be seen at close quarters
from the footpath alongside the Nottingham Canal by walking from
map reference SK 475/433 on the road from Ilkeston to Awsworth.

The Midland Counties Railway (later the Midland Railway) was 'born'
in Nottinghamshire at a meeting of coal-owners at the Sun Inn at
Eastwood 16 August 1832. The immediate desirability for the line was
to bring coal and minerals from the Erewash Valley to the growing
towns of the East Midlands, and the first section was opened from
Derby to Nottingham in 1839.

   Nottinghamshire experienced the 'railway mania' from the late 1840's
onwards, as did other parts of the country. This led to intense competition between the different companies, sometimes leading to duplication
of lines. As the Midland Railway had the virtual monopoly of the traffic around the Nottinghamshire and Derbyshire coal-field, the Great

Bennerley Viaduct.

Northern Railway was only able to claim access rights there in return for allowing the Midland to use Kings Cross station in London. However when the Midland Railway built its own London station at St. Pancras this arrangement ceased. This led in 1877 to the Great Northern extending one of its lines from Nottingham through Kimberley and Awsworth to Ilkeston and Derby. To do this the line had to cross the Midland Railway at Bennerley Junction. Because the ground where the viaduct was to cross was unstable, due to extensive mineral workings, a patent lattice wrought iron viaduct was designed to minimize the weight. This was known as the 'Warren' system, from a British patent taken out in 1848 by Captain James Warren who together with W.T. Manzoni had designed it.

The viaduct consisted of fifteen piers each of which had twelve wrought iron columns linked by bolted inter-laced ties. Work commenced in May 1876 and was completed in November 1877. It was used for the next ninety years but in 1968 the former Great Northern Railway line was closed. The embanked approaches were levelled to allow open-cast mining to take place on the land around and beneath the viaduct. British Rail made several planning applications to have the viaduct demolished to avoid the expense of having to maintain a structure for which there was no operational need. These applications were vigorously opposed by conservationists who pointed out that this was a structure of historic interest and was one of only two such viaducts still surviving.

After a public inquiry ordered by the Minister of the Environment, the viaduct was saved from demolition and in 1986 the Bennerley Viaduct Preservation Trust was set up to determine its future.

Places of Interest in the Neighbourhood
The Rod Not Spared (Bulwell)
Bad, Mad and Dangerous to Know (Hucknall)
From Whence the Phoenix Rose (Eastwood)

32 Bad, Mad and Dangerous to Know

Position: Hucknall, 7 miles north of Nottingham
O.S. Map: Nottingham & Loughborough area: Sheet No. 129: 1/50,000
Map Ref: SK 535/495
Access: Hucknall Market Place is on the A.611 road.

George Gordon Byron, born in 1788, became the sixth Lord Byron in
1798 when his great uncle the 'Wicked' fifth Lord died (see No.42).
He inherited the estate of Newstead with its Abbey, actually a former
priory of the Augustinian Canons. The family vault was in the parish
church of St. Mary Magdalene in Hucknall and it was here in 1824 that
the poet, the sixth Lord Byron was buried when he died at the age
of 36. His short life was an eventful one, and following his death in
Greece from a fever caught whilst helping the Greek insurgents to fight
the Turks his body was brought back to England, with his heart in
a separate urn. The body rested in Nottingham on the night of 15th
July and the funeral procession set out next morning for Hucknall.
The funeral itself was as dramatic as any incident in Byron's own life.
He had had a tempestuous love affair with Lady Caroline Lamb, who
wrote of him on their first meeting as 'bad, mad and dangerous to
know'. She later became ill with a hysterical fever and on the day of
Byron's funeral she was out riding in her carriage with her husband
William. He had to halt as the funeral procession passed and he asked
whose it was. In being told it was Lord Byron's he decided it would be
unwise to tell his wife. She did however hear later that night and col-
lapsed from shock.

The statue of him overlooking Hucknall Market Place is on the first
floor of a shop and is within a short distance from his burial place. The
statue was presented in memory of Byron in 1903 by Elias Lacey, a
signwriter and painter living in Hucknall who was an admirer of Byron.

Despite being buried, peace still eluded Byron. A parish clerk named
John Brown was said to have earned himself an additional income by
lowering a candle through a hole he had discovered in the vault and
charging the curious to inspect the coffins.

On 15th June 1938 Byron's rest was again disturbed, this time by
a more respectful party, including the Vicar, Churchwardens and
diocesan surveyor. They had obtained Home Office approval to break
into and inspect the vault for archaeological reasons. The proceedings
were carried out in great secrecy and photographs of contents taken.
The urn contained a plate with the inscription 'Within this urn are

Byron's statue in Hucknall Market Place.

deposited the heart and brain of Lord Noel Byron'.

Places of Interest in the Neighbourhood
The Rod Not Spared (Bulwell)
A Victorian Iron Monument (Bennerley)
From Whence the Phoenix Rose (Eastwood)

33 A Dark Satanic Mill

Position: Gonalston, 9 miles north-east of Nottingham
O.S. Map: Nottingham & Loughborough area: Sheet No. 129: 1/50,000
Map Ref: SK 679/469
Access: Gonalston is on the A.612 road, one mile north-east of its
junction with the A.6097 road.

The Gonalston Mill on the Dover Beck is one of many mills on the
Trent and its tributaries which in the 18th century was adapted from
grinding corn to spinning cotton.

The mill is well documented, largely because of a memoir by Robert
Blincoe published in Manchester as a pamphlet in 1832 as the *Memoir
of Robert Blincoe, an orphan boy, sent from the workhouse of St.
Pancras, London, at seven years of age to endure the horrors of a cotton
mill, through his infancy and youth, with a minute detail of sufferings.*
According to Blincoe, he and many other young boys and girls in the
workhouse were, in 1799, asked if they would like to become appren-
tices in a cotton mill in the country. There they would be fed on roast
beef and plum pudding, be allowed to ride on their masters' horses and
have silver watches and money in their pockets.

The reality was of course rather different. Conditions at Gonalston
Mill, owned by Ellice Needham, were described in detail by Blincoe.
Poor and insufficient food, long hours, inadequate clothing and lack of
medical attention meant that not only did the children lead wretched
lives but the mortality rate was high. So bad were conditions that news
of the childrens' treatment led to the St Pancras authorities who had
sent them to Gonalston setting up a committee of enquiry. Such
hardship was commonplace and in 1801 Parliament passed an Act to
protect Infant Paupers in Cotton Mills. A new apprentice house was
built, and gradually conditions improved.

Gonalston Mill still exists, until recently presenting a derelict and
forlorn appearance. Now however it has been converted into an attractive modern residence.

Places of Interest in the Neighbourhood
A Riverside Port (Fiskerton)
A Queen and a Sun-God (Thurgarton)

34 One Huge Folly

Position: Elston, 5 miles south-west of Newark
O.S. Map: Nottingham & Loughborough area: Sheet No. 129: 1/50,000
Map Ref: SK 747/483
Access: 120 yards along the road to Elston, on the south side of the A.46.

The Coeur de Lion restaurant and hotel has only been opened recently and the building is shown as Elston Towers on Ordance Survey maps. Built in 1874 and known according to the gate piers as Middleton House, it is described by Nicholas Pevsner as 'really one huge folly'.

It was built for Robert Middleton, and included a room designed for use as a Baptist Chapel. The house cost £30,000 to build, in the days when a normal sized house could be built for £50 or £100. Some of the stone used in its construction is said to have come from the old Trent Bridge at Nottingham which had been demolished a short time before.

After Robert Middleton died, the Towers later became the home of Joseph Truman who installed there a unique collection of furniture, some of which came from the Tuileries in Paris. The house suffered the indignity some years ago of becoming a maggot breeding factory with a tall steel chimney that did little to improve is appearance. Fortunately the chimney has now been demolished.

Places of Interest in the Neighbourhood
The Birds Have Flown (Sibthorpe)
7004 Killed in Battle (East Stoke)

The 'huge folly' of Elston Towers.

35 7004 Killed in Battle

Position: East Stoke, near Newark
O.S. Map: Mansfield & Worksop area: Sheet No. 120: 1/50,000
Map Ref: SK 747/501
Access: St. Oswald's Church is about half-a-mile along a narrow lane
(no through road) on the west side of the A.46 road 4 miles south of
Newark.

The 22nd August 1485 can be regarded as the end of the Middle Ages
and the beginning of modern England. It was on that day, at the Battle
of Bosworth Field that Henry Tudor, the leader of the Lancastrian
faction in the Wars of the Roses defeated Richard III, who was killed in
the battle, and became King Henry VII. Two years later on 16th June
1487 an epilogue to the Wars of the Roses was enacted in Nottinghamshire. The Battle of East Stoke was the culmination of a Yorkist
plot to unseat Henry VII and restore the throne to the House of York.
The intended new King was Lambert Simnel, the young pretender who
claimed to be the Earl of Warwick, and nephew of Richard III.

An army was raised by the Earl of Lincoln, regarded as the head of
the Yorkist party. It consisted of some 2,000 German mercenaries, together with some ill-armed Irish levies. After landing on 4th June 1487
in Lancashire, it marched south to Fiskerton (see No.36) a village two
miles from East Stoke, but on the opposite bank of the River Trent.

Henry VII and his army had in the meantime moved northwards and
on the 15th June had reached Radcliffe on Trent. The next morning
they marched up the old Roman Fosse Way (now the A.46) and made
contact with the enemy somewhere near East Stoke. The Yorkist
leaders were killed and their defeated troops tried to escape along the
track to the Fiskerton ferry. The narrow defile proved to be a trap and
so many were killed there that it became known as 'Red Gutter' from
the blood said to have flowed along it. Some 4,000 of the rebel troops
were thought to have been killed, as were 3,000 of the King's men.

To commemorate the 400th anniversary of the battle a simple stone
tablet was erected in the churchyard close to the south porch of
the church, recording the names of four who were killed and the
anonymous 7,000.

Places of Interest in the Neighbourhood
The Birds Have Flown (Sibthorpe)
One Huge Folly (Elston)

36 A Riverside Port

Position: Fiskerton, near Newark
O.S. Map: Mansfield & Worksop area: Sheet No. 120: 1/50,000
Map Ref: SK 736/510
Access: Fiskerton is about a mile from the railway station on the
Newark to Nottingham line. The minor road from Southwell runs
south-east from the A.612 road at Easthorpe.

Probably the most eventful time in Fiskerton's history was over 500
years ago when the rebel troops seeking to overthrow Henry VII
camped there before crossing the River Trent to fight the battle of East
Stoke (see No.35). Now a pleasant and peaceful riverside resort, it has
reminders of a more industrious past, if not exciting as in 1485. This
was in the days when the River Trent played an important part in the
economy of the East Midlands. The river had contributed to the
settlement in the region of the Anglo-Saxon tribes from the sixth
century onwards. After crossing the North Sea, they travelled up the
River Humber and the Trent, taking up residence at suitable points
near the rivers.

In later years the River Trent was the highway for two-way trade
when roads were a hindrance to the passage of goods rather than a help.
In the eighteenth century, with increasing trade, efforts were made to
provide transport by water along newly dug canals and existing rivers.
The Trent was useful for conveying coal and other minerals as well as
agricultural products from Nottinghamshire and Derbyshire and for
the supply of imported goods in the other direction.

Places of Interest in the Neighbourhood
A Dark Satanic Mill (Gonalston)
A Queen and a Sun-God (Thurgarton)

The riverside port of Fiskerton on the River Trent.

37 A Queen and a Sun-God

Position: Thurgarton, 3 miles from Southwell
O.S. Map: Nottingham & Loughborough area: Sheet 129: 1/50,000
Map Ref: SK 695/491
Access: Thurgarton is on the A.612 road, 2½ miles north-east of the junction with the A.6097 at Lowdham.

People in most English villages can usually rely on the church clock to tell them the time. Thurgarton has a rather different timepiece. It is situated on a roadside verge in the centre of the village and, as the inscription shows, it was erected in 1966. It is not the sort of clock one would expect to find in a rural area and in fact it came from number 4 platform on Nottingham's Midland Station. It was acquired and erected by Mr. R.C. Hoggard who lives at the adjoining Priory Farm, and was a railwayman for the whole of his working life.

The two barns which stand behind the clock also have features with a railway connection. On the end wall of each barn is a terracotta figure, one of Queen Elizabeth I and the other of Mithras, the sun-god of Persia. These were rescued by Mr. Hoggard from Hathern railway station when it closed, where they adorned a platform rockery. Hathern is a village in Leicestershire, but the railway station was in Sutton Bonington in Nottinghamshire, a mile away from the village from which it took its name.

The terracotta figures are made of what was known as Hathernware. In 1874 two brothers, George and James Hodson bought a plot of land near Hathern station and started the Hathern Station Brick Company. In 1890 the company started to make terracotta goods as well as bricks and turned out a great variety of chimney pots, urns, vases and decorative tiles.

The O.S. map reference of Hathern station site is SK 515/240 on Sheet 129.

Places of Interest in the Neighbourhood
A Riverside Port (Fiskerton)
A Dark Satanic Mill (Gonalston)

Queen Elizabeth and Mithras on barns at Thurgarton.

38 A Double Crossed Village

Position: Linby, 8 miles north of Nottingham
O.S. Map: Mansfield & Worksop area: Sheet No. 120: 1/50,000
Map Ref: SK 535/510
Access: Linby is on the east side of the A.611 road a mile north of Hucknall.

The village of Linby is unique in Nottinghamshire in having two crosses in the village street about a quarter of a mile apart. The one at the east end is known as the Bottom Cross and is built over a small stream. The other is of course known as the Top Cross. Just why there are two crosses is not known. Many villages have a cross around which a market was held but Linby is not recorded as having a market. The likeliest explanation for the existence of the Bottom Cross is that it was a marker cross delineating the boundary of Sherwood Forest. There are a number of perambulations of the Forest recorded, the earliest being 1505. Because Linby was on the River Leen, from which it derives its name, it is mentioned in the perambulations because the Leen marked the eastern boundary of the Forest.

If this is so the Bottom Cross would be regarded as royal property and the villagers might therefore have erected their own cross at the other end of the village. The Top Cross was broken when a writer on local matters visited the village in 1857 but it was repaired by 1869, as a metal plaque attached to it reads:

Restored June 16th, 1869
Andrew Montague, Armiger
John Lawrence Prior, Rector

Andrew Montagu was the owner of Papplewick Hall which had been built in about 1785, for the Hon. Frederick Montagu who had been a Privy Councillor. He died unmarried and the estate was passed down through the female line. Andrew, who succeeded his father in 1847 was born Andrew Wilson but in accordance with his grandfather's will, changed his surname to Montagu. This was done by royal licence which allowed the bearer to adopt the arms of the family. Hence Andrew Montagu was able to describe himself on the plate as 'armiger'.

Places of Interest in the Neighbourhood
A Pipe and a Crow's Feather (Selston)
An Ill-fated Family (Annesley)

39 From Where the Phoenix Rose

Position: Eastwood, 8 miles north-west of Nottingham
O.S. Map: Nottingham & Loughborough area: Sheet 129: 1/50,000
Map Ref: SK 478/469
Access: Greasley Beauvale Infants School, at the junction of Mill Road
and Dovecote Road, Eastwood. Dovecote Road is on the right hand
side of the Nottingham Road, B.6010, at Hill Top.

When the first steps to making education compulsory and available to
all were taken in the Education Act of 1870, local School Boards were
set up to carry out the work. Greasley School Board, one of over 40
such in Nottinghamshire, was started in 1878 and provided new schools
in its area. Most of the school buildings erected by these School Boards
have been demolished but two of those built by the Greasley Board still
survive, one at Kimberley, and the Greasley Beauvale Infants School at

Where D.H. Lawrence received his early education at Eastwood.

Eastwood. School Boards were discontinued in 1902 when their functions were taken over by local education authorities.

The plaque outside the Eastwood school, bearing his symbol of a phoenix, commemorates the fact that one of its most famous pupils, David Herbert Lawrence, attended the Beauvale Board School from 1893 to 1898. He was the son a miner and was born at Eastwood in 1885. His earlier novels, especially *Sons and Lovers*, are semi-autobiographical and contain many descriptions of Eastwood and the surrounding countryside, which in Lawrence's day had a number of collieries. The last of these closed recently and Eastwood is changing again, as it did in the nineteenth century when it became a mining town. Lawrence's birthplace in Victoria Street is now a museum depicting his earliest years. A leaflet *D.H. Lawrence Country* can be obtained from tourist information centres in the county and at Eastwood Library.

Places of Interest in the Neighbourhood
The Rod Not Spared (Bulwell)
A Victorian Iron Monument (Bennerley)
Bad, Mad and Dangerous to Know (Hucknall)

40 A Pipe and a Crow's Feather

Position: Selston, 7 miles south-west of Mansfield
O.S. Map: Mansfield & Worksop area: Sheet No. 120: 1/50,000
Map Ref: SK 458/533
Access: St. Helen's Church, Selston is on the western edge of the parish, on a minor road from the B.600 road at Selston Green.

Near the north-west corner of St. Helen's Church is a gravestone with the words:

> Dan Boswell
> Gypsy King
> 1737-1827
> I've lodged in many a town
> I've travelled many a year
> But death at last has brought me down
> To my last lodging here.

The stone is a comparatively new one and the original one was described in 1906 as being broken and only partly legible, with no verse inscribed on it. The church burial register records that Daniel Boswell was buried on 2nd March 1827 aged 76, not 90 as the stone claims. Selston Common was frequently used by gypsies so that it is probably why Dan Boswell was buried in the parish church.

The Boswell tribe of gypsies seems to have been a large one in Nottinghamshire. James Prior wrote a novel *Forest Folk* which contains much dialogue in the Nottinghamshire dialect and the word 'bos'll' is used as a term meaning gypsies in general.

At Newark Quarter Sessions on 4th October 1710 it was recorded rather gruesomely that seventy-six year old Thomas Boswile and his son Savidge were convicted as 'Sturdy Incorrigible Rogues' and ordered to have a large 'R' burnt into their left shoulder.

Some eight years after Daniel Boswell died another Boswell, Louis, died at Bestwood and was also described as King of the Gypsies. He was buried in the churchyard at Eastwood and in the burial register he was described as 'traveller' aged 42. There is a marginal note in the register signed F.W. Webb, Rector, 20 August 1909. It reads "This man known as the king of the Gypsies was interred in the presence of a 'vast concourse of spectators'. See Eastwood Parish Magazine for October 1909".

To the romantic writers of the nineteenth century, the gypsy king was a heroic figure to be celebrated in music and verse. William Howitt, a member of a Nottingham literary family wrote *The Rural Life of England* in 1836 and devoted a chapter to a description of gypsy life. He included a poem written by his brother Richard entitled 'The Gypsy King' in which he describes:

The slouching hat our hero wore
The Crown wherewith he King was crowned;
Wherein a pipe and a crow's feather
Were stuck in fellowship to-gether,
Was by a hundred winters browned.

Places of Interest in the Neighbourhood
A Double Crossed Village (Linby)
An Ill-fated Family (Annesley)

The reminder of former grandeur of Annesley Hall.

41 An Ill-fated Family

Position: Annesley, 8 miles north of Nottingham
O.S. Map: Mansfield & Worksop area: Sheet No. 120: 1/50,000
Map Ref: SK 517/511
Access: On the A.611 road, one and half miles south of the junction
with the A.608.

Probably few people speeding along the A611 road notice the solitary
gate pier of what was once the entrance to Annesley Hall. For three
hundred years it was the home of a family from Chaources in France
who came to England with William the Conqueror, their name being
eventually anglicised to Chaworth. George Chaworth acquired the Annesley estate by marriage in the eighteenth century. A descendant, William, was killed in a duel in 1765 by the fifth Lord Byron of nearby
Newstead (see No. 42).

As William Chaworth was unmarried, his estate passed to his cousin
George, who died without a male heir and his daughter Mary Ann
became the owner of Annesley Hall. She was only two years older than
the 6th Lord Byron, the poet, who as a boy inherited Newstead. He was
later to write:

> Now no more, the hours beguiling,
> Former favourite haunts I see,
> Now no more my Mary smiling
> Makes ye seem a heaven to me.

The Mary he mentions was Mary Chaworth and at the age of 15 he
declared his love for her. She preferred John Musters, to whom she was
already engaged and later married. She met an untimely death when,
after the 1831 Reform Bill was rejected, a riotous mob from
Nottingham set fire to the Musters seat at nearby Colwick. Mary took
refuge in the grounds, despite pouring rain and died shortly afterwards,
her illness no doubt accelerated by the exposure.

John Musters added the name Chaworth to his own and the
Chaworth-Musters family resided at Annesley Hall until about twenty
years ago. It was subsequently acquired by the Football Association
with a view to establishing a coaching centre, but its future is now
uncertain.

Places of Interest in the Neighbourhood
A Double Crossed Village (Linby)
A Pipe and a Crow's Feather (Selston)

42 Two Silly Forts

Position: Newstead Abbey, near Mansfield
O.S. Map: Mansfield & Worksop area: Sheet No. 120: 1/50,000
Map Ref: SK 540/539
Access: The entrance to Newstead Abbey is on the A.60 road, 4 miles
south of Mansfield and 10 miles north of Nottingham, map reference
SK 556/545.

Newstead Abbey, although ten miles from Nottingham and outside
the city, belongs to the City Council. It was purchased in 1931 and
presented to the City by a wealthy benefactor, Sir Julien Cahn. Just
over a hundred years earlier it had passed out of the hands of the Byron
family who had held it for 278 years. The last Byron to own it was the
poet and 6th Lord (see No.45).
   Newstead was a 12th century Augustinian priory which in 1539 was
granted by Henry VIII to Sir John Byron following the Dissolution of
the Monasteries. Parts of the priory buildings were destroyed and additions made to the remains to form a country residence, dignified by the
name of Abbey. The successive Byrons, one of whom, also Sir John,

The lake at Newstead.

was made a baron in 1643, attracted a number of soubriquets. One was known as 'Little Sir John with the Great Beard', and others were 'Foul-weather Jack' and 'Mad Jack'.

The most colourful of the Lords was undoubtedly the fifth, William, known as the 'Wicked'. In 1765 whilst dining with friends in a London tavern an argument developed which led Lord Byron to challenge William Chaworth to a duel. They retired to another room, where Chaworth was fatally wounded by Lord Byron's sword. He was tried by his peers in the House of Lords but though found guilty was able to evade punishment by claiming privilege as a peer.

The 'Wicked' Lord thereafter led a somewhat eccentric life, the effects of which can be seen at Newstead. In 1749 after he had re-shaped the upper lake he built two castellated forts on either side of the lake. The one on a hill above the lake was a tower with a gun emplacement known as 'Folly Castle'. The fifth Lord had been in the Navy in his younger days and he kept a twenty-gun ship on the lake which he used to indulge in mock battles. In the 1770's he altered the stables on the north-east side to make another castle or fort. It was these that prompted Sir Robert Walpole on a visit to Newstead to refer to them as 'two silly forts'.

The fifth Lord's eccentricity became something more serious in later life when he became reclusive and allowed the estate to deteriorate to such an extent that his great-nephew the sixth Lord, the poet, was com-pelled to sell it. The poet described the estate in verse:

> Through thy battlements, Newstead, the hollow winds whistle;
> Thou, the hall of my fathers, art gone to decay;
> In thy once smiling garden the hemlock and thistle
> Have choked up the rose which late bloomed in the way

Today, the Abbey and grounds combine as a museum and a delightful country park.

Places of Interest in the Neighbourhood
The Smallest Church (Blidworth)
Murdered for a Pair of Shoes (Harlow Wood)

71

43 A Warning from the Chief Constable

Position: Halloughton, near Southwell
O.S. Map: Mansfield & Worksop area: Sheet No. 120: 1/50,000
Map Ref: SK 689/517
Access: Halloughton is a mile and half south of Southwell on the west side of the A.612 road.

Manor Farm, Halloughton, presents a picturesque appearance with its medieval stone tower at the north end of the building. This is the earliest part of a house which has been added to over the centuries, and was originally built for defensive purposes.

It was formerly a prebendal house of the nearby collegiate church at Southwell, now the cathedral of the diocese. Prebendal houses were granted to canons of the collegiate church. In 1787, a historian reported that there had recently been some alterations carried out at the house. When a chimney stack was taken down many human skeletons, mostly of children, were discovered in a recess. An underground passage was discovered at the same time.

A notice board attached to the north wall of the house reads:

HALLOUGHTON
ALL VAGRANTS
Will be apprehended by Order of
The JUSTICES of the PEACE
J. Nicholson Chief Constable

The notice probably dates from the early years of the nineteenth century. The office of chief constable in those days was not the same as today, the head of a police force. Each hundred, a district of the county, had a high or chief constable, an unpaid duty which involved collecting the county rate from parish constables.

Places of Interest in the Neighbourhood
Birthplace of a Bull (Brackenhurst)
A Well-built Clean Town (Southwell)

44 Birthplace of a Bull

Position: Brackenhurst, near Southwell
O.S. Map: Mansfield & Worksop area: Sheet No. 120: 1/50,000
Map Ref: SK 695/523
Access: Brackenhurst is on the A.612 road a mile south of Southwell.

Situated on a hill with views over the surrounding countryside, Brackenhurst is now the home of a Nottinghamshire County Council college for training students in agriculture and food technology. The original mansion was built in 1828 for a clergyman, the Reverend Thomas C. Cane, vicar of Halloughton. On the 23 April 1861 Edmund Henry Hynam Allenby was born at Brackenhurst. His father Hynam Allenby had married Catherine Annie Cane, the daughter of the Reverend Thomas Cane, at Southwell Minster in 1859.

Edmund Allenby followed a military career and in the 1914-18 war rose to the rank of Field Marshal. After commanding the 3rd Army in France, he was appointed commander of the Egyptian Expeditionary Force. He was a man of considerable force of character, able to encourage those under him to emulate his drive and enthusiasm. He did however have a fierce temper which led to his being known as 'The Bull'. When he left his headquarters to visit his units, a mysterious coded message was telegraphed to them. This consisted merely of two letters 'B.L', which the recipients recognised as 'The Bull is Loose'.

The Field Marshal was created a viscount in 1919 and died in 1936. In 1973 a blue plaque was affixed to a wall of Brackenhurst, recording that he was born there.

Places of Interest in the Neighbourhood
A Warning from the Chief Constable (Halloughton)
A Well-built Clean Town (Southwell)

45 A Well-built Clean Town

Position: Southwell, 6 miles west of Newark
O.S. Map: Mansfield & Worksop area: Sheet 120: 1/50,000
Map Ref: SK 704/541
Access: From the junction of Westgate and Church Street, which form part of A.612, proceed along King Street for about 300 yards.

Southwell is rightly renowned for its magnificent Minster which, since 1888, has been the seat of the Bishop of the diocese. To its north and east, are a number of charming and elegant prebendal houses, each named after a prebend or parish which helped to administer the church.

About half a mile east of the Minister is another equally delightful part of Southwell known as Burgage Green, a large sloping grassed area with trees. On either side of the Green are some elegant eighteenth century houses. In one of these, Burgage Manor, the poet Lord Byron and his mother lived about 1810. He had been obliged to leave the ancestral home of Newstead Abbey because of the ruinous state in which he inherited it in 1798. It is appropriate that it was to Southwell that he and his mother moved because in 1789 Viscount Byng in his Torrington Diary described the town as "A well-built clean town such a one as a quiet distressed family ought to retire to; coals, provisions and religion to be had good and cheap".

Whilst it is unlikely that the old pump on the edge of Burgage Green supplied water for Lord Byron, he no doubt drank from a similar apparatus whilst staying in Southwell as a boy. This part of Southwell must have looked not much more different to him than it does to us today.

Places of Interest in the Neighbourhood
A Warning from the Chief Constable (Halloughton)
Birthplace of a Bull (Brackenhurst)

46 Who Kneads the Dough?

Position: Averham, near Newark
O.S. Map: Mansfield & Worksop area: Sheet No. 120: 1/50,000
Map Ref: SK 763/545
Access: Averham is on the A.617 road, 2 ½ miles west of Newark.

The small brick building to be seen in the village of Averham could be regarded as of minor importance. In fact it represents a part of village life which has largely disappeared. It was the parish oven, a communal facility which the villagers would use as an alternative to using costly fuel in their own homes.

The parish oven at Averham.

Ever since the reign of Elizabeth I the parish, as well as being the ecclesiastical unit, had played an important part in the administration of local services. The central Government had passed laws requiring each parish to provide for its own poor, aged, and infirm people, to repair its highways and to police itself. The duties were carried out largely without pay by men of the village on a rota basis. Whilst much would depend on the attitude of individual villagers as to how efficiently the duties were carried out, it would be apparent that other facilities could be provided on a communal basis. Besides ovens, some parishes had communal wash-houses, whilst services for farmers included mole and sparrow catching.

Places of Interest in the Neighbourhood
Diversions in the Market Place (Newark)
Mothering Sunday Revived (Coddington)
The Hall that Moved (Winthorpe)
Magnificent Perhaps, but not a Railway Station (Kelham)

The bull and bear baiting post at Newark.

47 Diversions in the Market Place

Position: Newark
O.S. Map: Lincoln: Sheet No. 121: 1/50,000
Map Ref: SK 779/539
Access: Newark Market Place, dominated by the spire of St. Mary Magdalen, is a quarter of a mile south-east of the junction of the A.6065 road with the Leicester to Lincoln road, the A.46.

The north-west corner of Newark's spacious market place contains two reminders of bygone days. One is a water-pump decorated with the town's coat of arms, whilst near to it is a wooden post with a chain and ring attached to it. This is a bull and bear-baiting post, an example of how our ancestors amused themselves. What today are regarded as barbaric sports seemed to have been accepted without qualms by the majority of people until comparatively recently.

   The use of such posts for tethering bears which were then attacked by dogs was clearly done to 'amuse' the spectators. Brown bears which had been native to Britain had died out and animals for baiting were imported. The use of the posts for baiting bulls, which no doubt attracted spectators, was thought to be necessary to improve the flavour of the meat. Dr. Charles Deering writing about Nottingham in 1751 said that the butchers in times past, whenever they had a mind to kill a bull, were obliged first to bait him in the Market Place, for which purpose there used to be a ring fixed in the ground and the mayoress had to find a rope to tether the bull. To meet the cost of the rope the mayoress was given a shilling by all who were granted the freedom of the town. He went on to say that the custom was no longer in use and the butchers had to pay 3s/4d (16p), called pin money for every bull they killed.

Places of Interest in the Neighbourhood
Who Kneads the Dough? (Averham)
Mothering Sunday Revived (Coddington)
The Hall that Moved (Winthorpe)
Magnificent Perhaps, but not a Railway Station (Kelham)

48 Mothering Sunday Revived

Position: Coddington, near Newark
O.S. Map: Lincoln: Sheet No. 121: 1/50,000
Map Ref: SK 835/545
Access: Coddington is on the A.17 road, two miles east of Newark.

In the churchyard at Coddington is a memorial to Constance Penswick Smith who died on the 10th June 1938 aged 60. She was the daughter of Charles Penswick and Mary C. Smith, her father being a former Vicar of Coddington. On the gravestone it is recorded that she was the founder of the movement for the revival of Mothering Sunday.

Miss Smith wrote a book entitled *Mothering Sunday* which was first published in 1921. In it, she gave an historical account of the festival which had traditionally been observed in the Christian church until it tended to disappear after about 1820. Celebrated on the fourth Sunday in Lent, it had evolved from the heathen festival 'when Winter has ended and Spring grows mild' in honour of the mother of the gods.

The Christian festival, although observed at the same time as the pagan one, had a deeper significance. It was of two-fold nature. Like today's observance it was intended to honour motherhood in general and to involve re-union of families who gathered together to honour their own mothers. In the north of England particularly it also had additional significance. Many parishes there were very large and when their population grew in areas some distance from the parish church, chapels or daughter churches were set up. The custom grew up therefore of a procession from the daughter churches to the mother church. The occasion was often accompanied by the baking of special confections, wafers or cakes, such as simnel cakes.

There had been some revivals of Mothering Sunday towards the end of the nineteenth century, but it was in 1914 that Miss Smith started a movement to revive the day as a religious festival. No formal society was formed but a headquarters was set up at 25 Regent Street, Nottingham. This was to organise the work of encouraging churches to revive the festival.

Places of Interest in the Neighbourhood
Who Kneads the Dough? (Averham)
Diversions in the Market Place (Newark)
The Hall that Moved (Winthorpe)
Magnificent Perhaps, but not a Railway Station (Kelham)

49 The Hall that Moved

Position: Winthorpe, 1 ½ miles north-east of Newark
O.S. Map: Lincoln: Sheet No. 121: 1/50,000
Map Ref: SK 812/566
Access: The village of Winthorpe can be reached in vehicles from either the A.46 road, on the west side 600 yards from the junction with the A.1 or from the A.1133 road 500 yards from its junction with the A.46.

The village hall at Winthorpe, despite the plaque dated 1874, has only been there since 1885. It had been situated at the nearby village of Brough, two miles further north along the A46 road. G.T. Pierce Duncombe, owner of Winthorpe Hall, had erected a church at Brough in 1874 in memory of his brother. In 1885 a new church was built at Brough and Mr. Duncombe purchased the original building. It was then re-erected in the grounds of Winthorpe Hall. It was used as a Sunday School, library and meeting-place for young men of the village.

In 1906 Mr. Duncombe sold the Hall, including the former church, to J.W. Need. Little use was made of the building until 1938 when Mr.

The village hall at Winthorpe.

Need presented it to the village. However, war was declared shortly afterwards and the hall was used by the military as a store.

In April 1951, after the hall had been de-requisitioned it was decided to modernise the former church so that it could be used for various activities. The village hall as it became known cost £830 to renovate. A tablet in the entrance recorded that it had been given by W.J. Need in 1938.

Places of Interest in the Neighbourhood
Who Kneads the Dough? (Averham)
Diversions in the Market Place (Newark)
Mothering Sunday Revived (Coddington)
Magnificent Perhaps, but not a Railway Station (Kelham)

50 Magnificent Perhaps, but not a Railway Station

Position: Kelham, near Newark
O.S. Map: Mansfield & Worksop area: Sheet No. 120: 1/50,000
Map Ref: SK 774/555
Access: The main entrance to Kelham Hall is on the A.617 road, 300 yards from the sharp bend in the road in the village.

It is perhaps a matter of opinion as to which is the greater curiosity, Kelham Hall itself or the tiny gazebo or summer house in the gardens. The Hall has undergone a number of alterations both in structure and in use since the eighteenth century. The Palladian house was built in about 1730 for the Manners-Sutton family. The Suttons had been extensive landowners in the vicinity, but when the male line died out, Kelham became the property of a Manners, a younger son of the Duke of Rutland, who added Sutton to his name.

The original building was burnt down in 1857 but an addition made in 1845 as a service wing survives on the north side of the present house, now the headquarters of the Newark and Sherwood District Council. The owner in 1857 was John Manners-Sutton, M.P. for Newark. When he decided to rebuild the Hall he employed the Victorian architect, Sir George Gilbert Scott. Scott was a leading exponent of the Gothic Revival movement in architecture and Kelham Hall is a good example of how he combined the ecclesiastical style of the original Gothic with a secular building. Unkind critics of Kelham Hall have been known to compare it to St. Pancras Station, which Gilbert Scott also designed. It certainly presents a curious appearance, asymmetrical, in red brick with stone dressings and an irregular skyline. Perhaps the most curious features are the windows of which there are twenty-three designs.

From a distance the summer house in the garden looks like the classical temple design of the eighteenth century found in many country house grounds, often as 'eye-catchers'. On closer inspection it is seen to be built of brick, instead of the classic stone, and has marble pillars similar to some in the Hall, so it would seem that Scott designed this too.

Places of Interest in the Neighbourhood
Who Kneads the Dough? (Averham)
Diversions in the Market Place (Newark)

(For illustration see Frontispiece)

51 Nodding Donkeys

Position: Dukes Wood, near Kirklington
O.S. Map: Mansfield & Worksop area: Sheet No. 120: 1/50,000
Map Ref: SK 677/602
Access: A public footpath through Dukes Wood starts at a point on a
minor road between Kirklington and Eakring. From Kirklington
proceed north-west along the A617 road for about half a mile. The
entrance to Dukes Wood is a mile and a half north along the Eakring
road.

Dukes Wood is now a site of scientific interest and is administered
by the Nottinghamshire Wildlife Trust. An information board at the
entrance gives details of the various types of vegetation and animal life
to be found in the wood. The 'animals' include three 'nodding donkeys'.
These are now idle but at one time it was possible to see the beams of

The donkey put out to grass in Duke's Wood.

these oil pumps slowly working up and down.

This part of Nottinghamshire may seem an unlikely competitor to Middle East states, but its oil made a valuable contribution to Britain's economy during the Second World War. Oil had been discovered in the area in the 1930s more or less by accident during exploration for new coal supplies. The first borehole started to produce oil a few weeks before the 1939-45 War started and by 1945 over 400,000 tons of oil had been produced. The work was carried out by British Petroleum and some 1200 people were employed. In 1942 in an effort to speed up production, representatives of B.P. went to the United States to buy more drilling rigs. This was not allowed under war-time legislation but contracts were entered into with two Oklahoma contractors for them to do the drilling. Accordingly, in February 1943, 42 American oilmen came to England to start work. They were housed for a time at Kelham Hall (see No.50) and then at a monastery nearby. The 'roughnecks' found it difficult to get used to Britains's war-time rations and so food for them was brought over from America. They remained in England for a year.

In 1991 a party of these oilmen returned to visit the sites where they worked nearly fifty years earlier. Whilst they were here a statue entitled 'Oil patch warrior' was unveiled in Dukes Wood by the Energy Secretary. It is a life-size representation of an oil rigger holding a huge spanner.

Places of Interest in the Neighbourhood
A Rector Shunned by his Flock (Eakring)
Rustic Revels (Wellow)
An Aristocratic Diplomat's Hobby (Rufford)

52 The Smallest Church

Position: Blidworth, near Mansfield
O.S. Map: Mansfield & Worksop area: Sheet No. 120: 1/50,000
Map Ref: SK 585/556
Access: Blidworth is on the B.6020 road, 5 miles east of its junction with the A.611 road.

The Church of St Mary of the Purification stands on a hill-top with wide views to the south. Most of the building only dates from 1739 but it has a number of features from the earlier medieval church. There are incised slabs used for surrounds of windows and a monument to a Sherwood Forest ranger from 1598.

The Churchyard also has remnants from earlier times as well as a more modern item. This is a model of a stone church, although not an exact replica of the main building. It was given to the church in 1963 by the man who had built it, William Tansley, a builder whilst his next-door neighbour, Mr. Cutmore made the windows.

Blidworth Church is well-known for its ancient custom, still carried on, of cradle rocking. Each year on the first Sunday in February the latest male child to have been baptised in the church is rocked in an old wooden cradle, decorated with flowers, as an act of rededication.

Places of Interest in the Neighbourhood
Two Silly Forts (Newstead Abbey)
Murdered for a Pair of Shoes (Harlow Wood)

The church in the church yard at Blidworth.

53 Murdered for a Pair of Shoes

Position: Harlow Wood, Near Mansfield
O.S. Map: Mansfield & Worksop area: Sheet No. 120: 1/50,000
Map Ref: SK 551/564
Access: Elizabeth Shephard's stone is on the east side of the A.60 road,
about half a mile north of the junction with the B.6020 road.

Elizabeth Shephard died aged 17 and had led an uneventful rural life
until she was murdered on 7 July 1817. Because of the way she met her
end she is remembered today by a road-stone recording her fate. Her
last resting place is close to the west tower of Papplewick Church where
a small stone has the simple inscription 'Elizabeth Shephard 1800-
1817'.

She had left home at Papplewick to go to Mansfield where she hoped
to be employed as a servant. She was wearing a pair of new shoes and
carried a light coloured umbrella. She was seen to leave Mansfield at six
o'clock the same day but did not return home. Her body was found next
morning by the side of the road, her skull having been fractured. The
weapon used, a large hedge stake, was found nearby.

On the 25th July, Charles Rotherham of Sheffield aged 33 years was
tried at the Shire Hall on a charge of murdering her. He had been
drinking at The Hut, a public house on the Mansfield road on the
evening of the murder. He stayed overnight at The Three Crowns Inn,
Redhill, where he had offered to sell a pair of ladies shoes and an
umbrella. Being unable to sell them he left the shoes in his bedroom and

The memorial to the girl murdered for her shoes at Harlow Wood.

later sold an umbrella in Bunny. News of these sales soon spread and he was arrested at Loughborough. After the coroner's inquest, he confessed to the crime and said he had no idea why he had done it. He did not know Elizabeth and did not speak, merely striking her repeatedly until she was dead. He then searched her body for money but finding none took the shoes and the umbrella.

He was executed three days after the trial, at Gallows Hill in Nottingham, the usual place for hangings. This was on the edge of the town, on Mansfield Road, near where today St. Andrew's Church stands. His body was taken to the Shire Hall where it was on public view, before being buried at the back of St. Mary's Church.

A Mr. Anthony Buckles and others from Mansfield paid for a stone to be erected near the place where the murder was committed. The stone when first erected had an ornament on top. It has recently been renovated so that the inscription can clearly be read.

Places of Interest in the Neighbourhood
Two Silly Forts (Newstead Abbey)
The Smallest Church (Blidworth)

The cross at Eakring where the Rev. William Mompesson preached.

54 A Rector Shunned by His Flock

Position: Eakring, 3 ½ miles S.E. of Ollerton
O.S. Map: Mansfield & Worksop area: Sheet 120: 1/50,000
Map Ref: SK 671/619
Access: On the east side of A.614, 2 ½ miles north of the junction with
A617, is the road to Eakring. On entering the village, Church Lane
leads to a track. About ¾ mile further on a footpath on the right leads
up a short flight of steps to the Mompesson monument.

In 1670 the Reverend William Mompesson was appointed Rector of
Eakring. He had previously been the Rector of Eyam in Derbyshire
where in 1665 the plague had decimated the population. To prevent the
plague spreading the Rector closed the village and continued minister-
ing to the dying, holding services in the open. His wife was one of the
victims of the disease.

When he came to Eakring, the villagers were afraid that he might have
brought the plague with him. He was not allowed to live in the village,
but found accommodation in a hut in Rufford Park. For a time he was
not allowed to conduct services in the church but held them in the open
at the isolated spot now called Pulpit Ash, where his monument was
erected by the first Lord Savile. It is a simple stone cross on a rough
hewn plinth surrounded by iron railings. A plaque records his story. He
was eventually accepted by the villagers and remained the incumbent
for 38 years.

Places of Interest in the Neighbourhood
Nodding Donkeys (Dukes Wood)
Rustic Revels (Wellow)
An Aristocratic Diplomat's Hobby (Rufford)

55 Under the Spreading Chestnut Tree

Position: Carlton-on-Trent
O.S. Map: Lincoln: Sheet No. 121: 1/50,000
Map Ref: SK 779/640
Access: Carlton-on-Trent is on the A.1 road 6 miles north of Newark.

The smithy was once an essential feature of English village life. It was here that all sorts of iron agricultural implements were made and repaired. The smithy therefore came to be regarded as a community meeting point, for the exchange of news and gossip.

The smith was one of the most respected men of the village, due to his skill, acquired only after a long apprenticeship, and physical strength. He also had powers denied to other men. They could not mount a horseshoe with the points downwards without risking ill-luck. The blacksmith was not subject to such a hazard and so the smithy could be decorated on the outside with a giant size horseshoe with the points downwards. Such is the one at Carlton-on-Trent as well as one at Gonalston (see No.33), both of which are adorned also with the poetic advertisement:

> Gentlemen, as you pass by,
> Upon this shoe pray cast an eye,
> If it be too strait I'll make it wider,
> I'll ease the horse and please the rider.
> If lame from shoeing as they often are
> You may have them eased with
> The Greatest Care.

Places of Interest in the Neighbourhood
Stay Away from my Door (Girton)
A Queen Who Died in Nottinghamshire (Harby)

56 A Pomegranate Tells the Time

Position: Ossington

O.S. Map: Mansfield & Worksop area: Sheet No. 120: 1/50,000

Map Ref: SK 759/652

Access: The village of Ossington is on a minor road starting at Kneesall on the A.616 road and at Carlton on Trent on the A.1 road. The church of Holy Rood stands to the north of the village and is reached by a track commencing a quarter of a mile east.

The church at Ossington is in a quiet secluded position surrounded by trees and the former garden of Ossington Hall, demolished in 1963. In the churchyard stands the baluster sundial made in 1812 by

Baluster sun-dial at Ossington.

Arthur Buckle. The word 'baluster' is derived from an Italian word for the blossom of the wild pomegranate, which resembles in shape the cylindrical form of a baluster.

Ossington Hall was built in the eighteenth century and was the home of the Cartwright family, one of whom, Edmund, was the inventor of the power loom. When the sundial was erected, the Denisons, wool merchants from Leeds, owned the Hall. William Denison who bought the Hall is said to have made his fortune by one ship's cargo, the ship arriving at Lisbon immediately after an earthquake in 1753. In 1812 the owner was John Wilson, a nephew of the previous Denison owner, who on inheriting the estate changed his name to Denison. His son, John Evelyn Denison became Speaker of the House of Commons and was created Viscount Ossington.

Places of Interest in the Neighbourhood
England's Last Open Field Village (Laxton)
Education on a Tight Budget (Normanton-on-Trent)

Girton's reminder of the unwelcome visits of the River Trent.

57 Stay Away from My Door

Position: Girton, 8 miles north of Newark
O.S. Map: Lincoln: Sheet No. 121: 1/50,000
Map Ref: SK 825/662
Access: Girton lies on the west side of the A.1133 road and the church of St. Cecilia is in the centre of the village.

Although the village of Girton is over half a mile from the River Trent it has or had the misfortune to have a small tributary, the River Fleet much nearer. It was no doubt that this caused the waters of the Trent, when the river was swollen with heavy rain or melted snow from upstream, to flood the village. As the stone plaque on the churchyard wall records this has happened on at least four occasions between 1705 and 1947.

   The plaque was originally on the wall of a house in the village. It was the idea of a man called G. Porter, his initials being shown at the bottom of the plaque together with the words:

> When this you see
> Pray think of me

After the disastrous flood of 1974, which affected the City of Nottingham as well as the surrounding countryside, considerable works were carried out which so far have prevented serious flooding.

Places of Interest in the Neighbourhood
Under the Spreading Chestnut Tree (Carlton-on-Trent)
A Queen Who Died in Nottinghamshire (Harby)

58 England's Last Open Field Village

Positon: Laxton, near Ollerton
O.S. Map: Mansfield & Worksop area: Sheet No. 120: 1/50,000
Map Ref: SK 724/671 (Visitors' Centre)
Access: From Ollerton take the A.6075 road for two miles, then at a sharp left-hand turn, straight ahead on a minor road for two and a half miles.

The open-field system of farming was extensively developed in Midland England from the Middle Ages. Villages had two or three large unhedged and unfenced fields which were divided into strips or furlongs. Each farmer was allocated a number of strips, usually separated to ensure that each farmer had lands of more or less equal value, as some parts would be more fertile than others.

The system was not the most efficient one, involving individual farmers in much travelling between strips. When improved methods of agriculture were introduced, particularly in the eighteenth century, the opportunity was taken to discontinue the strips and enclose them in separate fields with hedges. At Laxton, although some enclosure took place, the open-field system has been retained to this day. This unique system is regulated by a survival of medieval manorial government, the Court Leet. It meets each year and appoints a jury to control the cultivation of the open fields.

The Visitors' Centre provides information on how this system works and on what to see in the village.

Places of Interest in the Neighbourhood
A Pomegranate Tells the Time (Ossington)
Education on a Tight Budget (Normanton-on-Trent)

59 Rustic Revels

Position: Wellow, near Ollerton
O.S. Map: Mansfield & Worksop area: Sheet No. 120: 1/50,000
Map Ref: SK 670/661
Access: Wellow is on the A.616 road, a mile and a half south east of Ollerton.

Wellow presents a scene reminiscent of the traditional picture of the English village, with its green, its red-roofed cottages and the tall maypole. Not so traditional is the material from which the maypole is made, steel. The present one, 55 feet high, was specially made in 1976 to replace an earlier wooden one. It has a cockerel on the top as a weather vane and is the tallest permanent maypole in England.

Wellow Maypole.

The previous maypoles were made of wood, and were provided by the Savile family from their estate at nearby Rufford (see No.60). A.W. Savile presented one in 1887 to celebrate Queen Victoria's Diamond Jubilee. This lasted until 1923 when it was replaced by one acting as a memorial to the men from Wellow killed in the First World War. Ten feet were lopped off the top during the 1939-45 war, because it had become unsafe, and it was replaced in 1950, when the traditional ceremonies were revived.

The custom of crowning the May Queen and of children dancing around the maypole, holding on to the garlands, seems to have originated as a celebration of the coming of summer and may date back to pagan times. Just why the ceremonies have survived at Wellow and few other places is a mystery. The tradition is certainly strong there for despite breaks caused by two world wars, the celebrations are carried out with undimmed enthusiasm, now on the Spring Bank Holiday.

Places of Interest in the Neighbourhood
Nodding Donkeys (Dukes Wood)
A Rector Shunned by his Flock (Eakring)
An Aristocratic Diplomat's Hobby (Rufford)

The fountain copied from an antique lamp at Rufford.

60 An Aristocratic Diplomat's Hobby

Position: Rufford Country Park, 1 ½ miles south of Ollerton
O.S. Map: Mansfield & Worksop area: Sheet No. 120: 1/50,000
Map Ref: SK 646/647
Access: The entrance to Rufford Country Park is on the A.614 road, 4 miles north of the junction with A.617.

Just behind the orangery in Rufford Park is a replica of an antique lamp discovered in excavations carried out at Civita Lavinia in Italy. The excavations were instigated by John Savile when he was the Ambassador in Rome from 1883 to 1888.

He and his four brothers were the illegitimate sons of the 8th Earl of Scarborough, their mother being usually called Agnes Lumley. She was described as 'a French lady who had been banished somewhat roughly from the home of her husband in her native country'.

John Savile was created Baron Savile of Rufford in 1888 and lived at the family seat of Rufford Abbey until he died there in 1896. Rufford Abbey had been built as a country house on the site of a former Cistercian Abbey, but most of the house was demolished in 1959. The remaining buildings and park are now owned by Notts. County Council. The country park has many attractive features including a lake, woodland walks, exhibition and craft centres and restaurants.

Places of Interest in the Neighbourhood
Nodding Donkeys (Dukes Wood)
A Rector Shunned by his Flock (Eakring)
Rustic Revels (Wellow)

61 The Heart of the County

Position: Edwinstowe near Ollerton
O.S. Map: Mansfield & Worksop area: Sheet No. 120: 1/50,000
Map Ref: SK 628/663
Access: The Dukeries Hotel is on the B.6034 road, one and a quarter miles north-west of the junction with the A.614 road.

Edwinstowe represents three of Nottinghamshire's most important characteristics. It owes its name and historic importance to the year A.D.632, when King Edwin of Northumbria was killed in battle, and according to an unproven legend was secretly buried in the forest.

For the next 1200 years or so Edwinstowe remained a small village in the heart of Sherwood Forest, with agriculture as the main occupation, together with crafts associated with the forest. The coming of the railway in the 1840's opened up the surrounding countryside, the Dukeries, to visitors. The village schoolmaster in 1890 complained that "Edwinstowe is becoming more and more a holiday resort with the usual result".

The influx of visitors until 1896 came by train to Worksop and from there travelled by horse-brake. In 1896 Edwinstowe's own railway station was opened and this no doubt influenced the building of the Dukeries Hotel in 1898. This was much grander than the public houses in the village and contained a large ballroom. The doorway was decorated with carvings of foresters and Robin Hood and his men. The Hotel was burned down in 1929 but was rebuilt, the carved figures being preserved.

A third string was added to Edwinstowe's bow in 1925 when the first steps were taken to build a colliery. This meant a considerable increase in population. Today there is still some agriculture in and around Edwinstowe, but tourism and mining are of more importance. A visitor's centre near the famed Major Oak recalls the Glory of Sherwood Forest.

Places of Interest in the Neighbourhood
A Ducal Folly (Clipstone)
A First Class Mail Box (Budby)

The forester blowing his own trumpet at Edwinstowe.

62 A Ducal Folly

Position: Archway Lodge, between Warsop and Edwinstowe
O.S. Map: Mansfield and Worksop area: Sheet 120: 1/50,000
Map Ref: SK 607/659
Access: On the south side of the A.6075 road, just under a mile and a quarter from the junction with B.6035, is a bridle path. The Lodge is about 600 yards along the tree-lined track.

Archway Lodge can be approached from one of two directions, both along a rough track. From either direction the appearance of the Lodge presents the unsuspecting traveller with a sharp contrast to the rural surroundings. The large building with an archway through it is distinguished by the carved figures on it. These represent one real person, Richard Coeur-de-Lion, whilst the others are appropriately enough of the legendary band of outlaws associated with Sherwood Forest, the Lodge being in the heart of the former Royal forest. They include Robin Hood, Friar Tuck, Maid Marion and Little John.

The Lodge was built for the fourth Duke of Portland in 1844 and was based on the gatehouse leading to Worksop Priory. Intended primarily as a hunting lodge, it also had a schoolroom over the archway. In 1864, at a time when Clipstone was the poorest village in the county, it was described as being 'free to all the poor girls in Clipstone'.

The Lodge owes its isolation to the Duke's intention that it should mark the start of a twenty-mile rural drive to Nottingham. This scheme, although it never came to fruition, was typical of his ambitious plans to improve this part of his extensive estates. He was a man of great physical energy with numerous interests. His father the 3rd Duke, Prime Minister in 1783, had inherited the Welbeck Estate and had done much to improve the sandy wastes. The 4th Duke, on inheriting the title came to live at Welbeck and created fertile water meadows between Mansfield and Clipstone by using the River Maun to make what became known as the 'Duke's Flood Dyke'.

Places of Interest in the Neighbourhood
The Heart of the County (Edwinstowe)
A First Class Mail Box (Budby)

Clipstone Arch, a ducal folly.

63 A First Class Mail Box

Position: Budby, near Ollerton
O.S. Map: Mansfield & Worksop area: Sheet No. 120: 1/50,000
Map Ref: SK 618/701
Access: Budby is on the A.616 road, 3 miles north-west of the Ollerton
roundabout junction with the A.614 road.

The village of Budby is divided by the A.616 road. A short distance
away on the west side stands an unusual mail box. It is hexagonal
in shape unlike the more usual cylindrical shape. The latter replaced
the hexagonal ones because they were considered to be a hazard, the
straight sides being likely to trap letters.

Hexagonal letter boxes were introduced in 1865 and were known
as Penfold types after the designer J.W. Penfold, an architect and
surveyor. They were made in three sizes and those for urban areas
had apparatus inside which led to the complaints about letters being
mislaid. The rural area boxes did not have this apparatus, which
perhaps explains why Budby's has survived. Its use would have been
minimal as the population never exceeded 130.

Places of Interest in the Neighbourhood
A Ducal Folly (Clipstone)
The Heart of the County (Edwinstowe)

The 'Penfold' pillar-box at Budby.

64 An Unusual Churchyard Tree

Position: Cuckney, near Worksop
O.S. Map: Mansfield & Worksop area: Sheet No. 120: 1/50,000
Map Ref: SK 566/714
Access: Cuckney is on the A.60 road, 6 miles south of Worksop, near the junction with the A.616 road.

It is unusual to find a 'sequoia gigantea' Wellingtonia tree in an English churchyard. The one in Cuckney churchyard is explained by a metal plaque at the base of the tree, although it is hidden by the lower branches. The plaque records that the tree was presented to her Grace, the Duchess of Portland D.B.E. on the 30th November 1963. The occasion was the 21st anniversary of the founding of the Norton-Cuckney and District Gardens and Village Produce Association.

   In 1942 when the Produce Association was formed the growing of as much food as possible in England was paramount. The Second World War had been in progress for three years and England could no longer rely on overseas supplies of food. The Duchess of Portland, wife of the 7th Duke, had then been president of the Association for 10 years. At the planting ceremony the Duchess said the sequoia tree was four years old and had been grown from a seed in the Welbeck Estate gardens. In America such trees grow to a height of 300 feet, but in the English climate growth is restricted. The Duchess hoped that the Produce Association would last as long as the tree itself.

Places of Interest in the Neighbourhood
A Man of the Turf Turned Politician (Norton)
A Lonely Self-Isolated Man (Welbeck)
Where Rhinoceros and Hippopotamus Roamed (Creswell)

The Bentinck Memorial fountain near Norton.

65 A Man of the Turf Turned Politician

Position: Norton, 4 ½ miles south of Worksop
O.S. Map: Mansfield & Worksop area: Sheet 120: 1/50,000
Map Ref: SK 583/720
Access: From the B.6034 road, 1 ½ miles north of its junction with A.616, is a road running west to Norton. On the north side of the road, 1 ½ miles along, is the Bentinck Memorial.

The walk along the road to Norton, with woods on one side and Welbeck Park with its lake on the other is a pleasant one, especially in the summer. It was however to prove fatal to Lord George Frederick Bentick. On 21st September 1848 he set out on foot from Welbeck, intending to dine with Earl Manvers at Thoresby. He never arrived, dying suddenly at the spot where the memorial to him stands.

He was born in 1802, the son of the 4th Duke of Portland who built Archway Lodge (see No.62). He served as a major in the army and when his aunt married George Canning he became his secretary. Following Canning's death when Prime Minister in 1827, Lord George became M.P. for Lyme Regis, a position he held until his death. For the first fifteen years as an M.P. he seldom spoke in the House of Commons, spending more time indulging his passion of horse racing. However, one of the burning political questions of the day changed him completely. The Corn Laws which protected the price of the home grown cereal against foreign imports became a major issue in the 1840's. When the Prime Minister, Sir Robert Peel announced his support for free trade, his opponents, the protectionists, asked Lord George to take the lead in opposing the repeal of the Corn Laws. He thereupon sold his racing stud and devoted himself to the cause with vigour, showing undisclosed talent as an orator. His sudden death cut short what would have probably been a successful political career.

A second statue to his memory stands in Mansfield Market Place.

Places of Interest in the Neighbourhood
An Unusual Churchyard Tree (Cuckney)
A Lonely Self-Isolated Man (Welbeck)
Where Rhinoceros and Hippopotamus Roamed (Creswell)

66 A Lonely Self-Isolated Man

Position: Welbeck Abbey, near Worksop
O.S. Map: Mansfield & Worksop area: Sheet No. 120: 1/50,000
Map Ref: SK 588/755
Access: Welbeck Abbey itself is not open to the public, as it is mainly an
Army College but there is a public footpath through the estate, part of
Robin Hood Way. This starts on the B.6034 road at map ref. SK
597/758 and continues for 2 miles westwards.

Welbeck Abbey is the name given to a mansion erected or altered at
various times from the seventeenth century onwards. There are still a
few remnants of the original abbey founded in 1153-4. At the dissolution of the monasteries the estate passed into private ownership, eventually to Sir Charles Cavendish. His son became the Duke of Newcastle
and from a descendant's marriage into the Bentinck family, Welbeck
became the home of successive Dukes of Portland. It was the 5th Duke,
William John Cavendish-Scott-Bentinck who introduced a number of
curiosities into the Welbeck Estate.

Lady Ottoline Morrell, a step-sister of the 6th Duke of Portland,
described the 5th Duke as "so absorbed with his vast work of digging
out the underground rooms and tunnels that he was oblivious of
everything else. He pursued this hobby without any idea of beauty, a
lonely self-isolated man". It was a 'hobby' that included building an
underground tunnel from the Abbey to the railway station so that he
could travel in a closed private waggonette on the railway, thus ensuring privacy.

The underground ballroom which he built and the miniature railway
track from the kitchens were perhaps not as eccentric as is commonly
supposed. The ballroom is lit naturally by sky-lights and the kitchen
transport probably kept the food hot.

The reminders of the 5th Duke which can still be seen also include the
numerous neo-Tudor lodges in various parts of the estate. The ven-
tilators to the underground pigsties and laundries in the lodge gardens
are indeed curious, like giant mushrooms, and if built today would no
doubt be welcomed as environmentally 'green'.

Places of Interest in the Neighbourhood
An Unusual Churchyard Tree (Cuckney)
A Man of the Turf turned Politician (Norton)
Where Rhinoceros and Hippopotamus Roamed (Creswell)

67 Where Rhinoceros and Hippopotamus Roamed

Position: Creswell Crags, near Worksop
O.S. Map: Mansfield & Worksop area: Sheet No. 120: 1/50,000
Map Ref: SK 537/742
Access: Four and half miles south-west of Worksop, take the B.6042
road eastwards from its junction with the A.616 road.

The tiny Millwood Brook forms the boundary between Nottinghamshire and Derbyshire for part of its course. At Creswell Crags it
broadens out into a lake, with Nottinghamshire on its southern side. It
forms a picturesque scene, with crags, dotted with caves, rising up on
either side. There is little to indicate to the casual observer that this is
one of the most important sources of information about life in
prehistoric England. For it is in the caves and rock-shelters along both
sides of the lake that evidence of life in the later Palaeolithic period,
about 10,000 years ago, has been found.

Excavations were first begun in 1874 when Sir William Boyd Dawkins
and the Reverend Magens Mello explored the caves which were given
the names of Church Hole, on the Nottinghamshire side, and Robin
Hood's Cave, the Pin Hole and Mother Grundy's Parlour on the Derbyshire side. Later excavations brought to light numerous treasures,
many of which are now in the British Museum. One of these was a piece
of smooth bone three inches long and an inch deep on which had been
scratched the head and shoulders of a horse, with the hair of its mane
standing up straight. Another interesting find showed a masked man
executing a ceremonial dance. The excavations also discovered bones
which belonged to the hippopotamus, rhinoceros and hyena, thus establishing that this part of the world once had a much warmer climate.

In 1976 the Nottinghamshire and Derbyshire County Councils joined
together in setting up the Visitor's Centre. For the next four years, new
excavations took place which revealed much new information about
the changes which had taken place at Creswell Crags. The result of
these explorations and studies are explained in an interesting way in the
Centre.

Places of Interest in the Neighbourhood
An Unusual Churchyard Tree (Cuckney)
A Man of the Turf turned Politician (Norton)

68 Education on a Tight Budget

Position: Normanton-on-Trent
O.S. Map: Mansfield & Worksop area: Sheet No. 120: 1/50,000
Map Ref: SK 791/690
Access: Normanton-on-Trent is two miles east of the B.1164 road, along a minor road a mile and a half south of Tuxford.

In 1776 when Henry Jackson had a school built opposite the church at Normanton-on-Trent the population probably numbered about 250. The number of children must have been small, but most would have qualified for his wish that the school be used to educate ten poor children. The plaque attached to the building, now a house, records that he also endowed the school with £4 a year.

The school received a further increase in income in 1781 when a Mrs. Hall bequeathed land for the purpose which fifty years later produced £9 a year in rent. The village seems to have been particularly fortunate in the eighteenth century in receiving benefactions for the poor. In 1781 two houses for poor women were built and nine years later almshouses for four poor women were added.

Places of Interest in the Neighbourhood
England's Last Open Field Village (Laxton)
A Pomegranate Tells the Time (Ossington)

The former school at Normanton-on-Trent.

69 A Queen who Died in Nottinghamshire

Position: Harby, 12 miles N.E. of Newark
O.S. Map: Lincoln: Sheet 121: 1/50,000
Map Ref: SK 879/705
Access: Harby lies in a small peninsula of Nottinghamshire which is surrounded on three sides by Lincolnshire. It is only half a mile from the Lincolnshire border. It is about 5 miles from the A.1133, through Wigsley.

In 1290 Queen Eleanor, wife of Edward I, died at the house of Richard de Weston in Harby. She had been taken ill in September whilst accom-

Queen Eleanor is remembered at Harby.

panying the King on one of his visits to the East Midlands and died two months later. Eleanor of Castile, the daughter of Ferdinand III married Edward, the son of Henry III in 1254 when Edward was 15. She accompanied Edward on the last Crusade where she is reputed to have saved his life by sucking poison from a wound.

After her death, the body was brought to London for burial in Westminster Abbey, a journey of 130 miles which in those days took several days. At the various places where the cortège stayed overnight on its way to London, nine crosses were later erected. These became known as Eleanor Crosses, the last one being Charing Cross in London. There is no Eleanor Cross at Harby but the church of All Saints, completed in 1876, has a statue of Queen Eleanor in a niche on the east wall of the tower.

An information board near the church gives something of the village's history.

Places of Interest in the Neighbourhood
Under the Spreading Chestnut Tree (Carlton-on-Trent)
Stay Away from My Door (Girton)

The 'lock-up' at Tuxford.

70 Overnight Accommodation

Position: Tuxford
O.S. Map: Mansfield & Worksop area: Sheet No. 120: 1/50,000
Map Ref: SK 735/710
Access: Tuxford now lies on the B.1164 road. The lock-up is a short
distance south of the junction with the A.6075 road, on the road to
Egmanton.

Before the establishment of full time paid police forces, law and order
was the responsibility of the parish constable. Until an offender could
be brought before a justice of the peace they needed to be lodged somewhere safe, particularly if violent or drunk. A number of places, including Tuxford, had lock-ups built for this purpose.

In 1823 when the Tuxford lock-up was built, the town had over
one thousand inhabitants and was a busy market town. Moreover it
was directly on the Great North Road and was a stopping-place for
travellers. To accommodate them there were nine hotels, inns and
taverns. These together with the comings and goings of travellers and
the markets and fairs no doubt caused a certain amount of minor
crimes. The lock-up became redundant when a county police station
was built, but is now retained as an ancient monument.

Places of Interest in the Neighbourhood
A Tale of Two Churches (Milton)
A Lady Called Saunchia (Rampton)
Murder in the Jockey House (Gamston)

71 A Tale of Two Churches

Position: Milton, 2 miles north-west of Tuxford
O.S. Map: Mansfield & Worksop area: Sheet 120: 1/50,000
Map Ref: SK 715/730
Access: From the Markham Moor intersection on the A.1, 2 miles north of Tuxford, a minor road on the south-west side leads to Milton village. About 700 yards past a left hand turn, a road on the left leads to the Mausoleum in about 300 yards.

The fourth Duke of Newcastle married Georgiana Mundy of Shipley, Derbyshire in 1807. The Duchess had fourteen children but died in giving birth to the last of them, twins, in 1827. She is said to have expressed a wish to be buried on a hill on which she saw the sun shining from her residence at Clumber. As the Duke owned the land he decided to build a mausoleum there as the Duchess's last resting-place. The Greek Doric building, of Roche Abbey stone, was designed by Sir Robert Smirke, who designed the British Museum and it was consecrated in 1834. The Duke obtained permission for the new building to be used as the parish church, in place of the existing All Saints at West Markham a quarter of a mile away. The name of the parish was changed to Markham Clinton, Clinton being the family name of the Duke. He had the road to West Markham planted with alternate lime trees and Lombardy poplars.

All Saints Church at West Markham is also well worth a visit. It is a quarter of a mile east of Milton, map reference SK 721/724. The west gable has an unusual weatherboarded turret whilst inside are some old oak benches and a font with rather fierce looking figures carved on it. The original beaten earth floor still forms part of the nave, and the atmosphere of this small church is very much as it must have been centuries ago.

Places of Interest in the Neighbourhood
Overnight Accommodation (Tuxford)
Murder in the Jockey House (Gamston)
A Lady Called Saunchia (Rampton)

72 Murder in the Jockey House

Position: Gamston, south-west of Retford
O.S. Map: Mansfield and Worksop: Sheet 120: 1/50,000
Map Ref: SK 686/766
Access: Half a mile along Jockey Lane which is 1 mile north of Elkesley, on the east side of the A.1.

Today Jockey Lane is a quiet, narrow country lane. In the eighteenth century, as the milestone known as the Jockey Stone shows, it was the coach road to Worksop Manor House. The stone stands at the junction with what was then the old road to London which connected with the Great North Road. The milestone was known as the Jockey Stone because it was opposite the Jockey House. This building, later a farmhouse, was an inn in the eighteenth century, at what was a busy

The milestone near the Jockey House.

cross-roads.

In 1721 a company of Guards was changing barracks and stopped for refreshment at the Jockey House. Their commanding officer, Midford Hendry, became involved in a political argument with another man in the inn, John Baragh. The argument became violent and Hendry drew his sword, killing Baragh by stabbing him through the heart. John Baragh was buried in the churchyard at the nearby village of Elkesley where his tombstone recorded that he was aged 29 and a 'gentleman'. The entry in the burial register reads that he was 'stabed'.

Places of Interest in the Neighbourhood
A Tale of Two Churches (Milton)
Overnight Accommodation (Tuxford)
A Lady Called Saunchia (Rampton)

Tudor gate-way at Rampton.

73 A Lady Called Saunchia

Position: Rampton
O.S. Map: Mansfield & Worksop area: Sheet No. 120: 1/50,000
Map Ref: SK 800/786
Access: Rampton is four miles north of the A.57 road, on a minor road
starting a hundred yards east of the A.6075 road.

The elaborate gateway to the right of Rampton church was built in the
Tudor period and is all that is left of the buildings of successive lords of
the manor. It was the private entrance into the churchyard from the
Manor House. The gateway is adorned with terracotta panels containing the coats-of-arms of the various owners of the Manor and Hall.
These include the first owner in the twelfth century who took his name
from the village. The Maulords, Stanhopes, Babingtons and Eyres were
the subsequent owners. They were in fact all descendants of the first
owner, Robert de Rampton. The properties subsequently passed down
through the female line when there was no male heir.

In 1520 Saunchia Stanhope, aged seven years and five months, was
married to John Babington, who was not much older. When her father
died in 1527, his property passed through trustees to John when he
became 21. In 1541 John and Saunchia sold parts of other estates they
owned at Tuxford and Laxton. It is most likely that the proceeds of
these sales was the source of finance for the gateway.

The name 'Saunchia' is Spanish and is the same as the Latin 'Sanctus',
holy. In the register of baptisms the Christian name of 'Sench' occurs as
a girl's Christian name. There were baptisms of this name in 1582 and
1584. This was no doubt a name adopted by parishioners as a tribute to
the lady of the manor. Whether it was spelled that way deliberately or
because the tenants would have been unlikely to have seen the name
written is a matter for conjecture.

Places of Interest in the Neighbourhood
Overnight Accommodation (Tuxford)
A Tale of Two Churches (Milton)
Murder in the Jockey House (Gamston)

74 An Early Disinfecting Station

Position: Retford
O.S. Map: Mansfield & Worksop area: Sheet No. 120: 1/50,000
Map Ref: SK 705/811
Access: Retford Market Place lies between the A.620 and A.638 roads.

The Broad Stone today stands in front of the Town Hall in Retford
Market Place. It has however occupied at least two other sites and
whilst something is known of its uses, its origin is not certain. In its
present position it is the inverted base of a cross which at one time stood
at a site known as Dominie Cross. It is thought that this may have been
the marker of a point beyond which the townspeople were forbidden to
proceed when the town was suffering from an outbreak of plague in
1451.

Another theory is that in times of plague the market was held around
the stone. The country people who brought their produce for sale
thought that the disease could be caught by contact with others, so they
would lay out their goods for the towns folk to buy. Payment was made
by dropping coins in the hollow top of the stone which was filled with
vinegar to disinfect the money.

By the early part of the nineteenth century the stone had been moved
to the centre of the market place. Here it was the scene of much
agitation in the nineteenth century for around the stone was erected the
hustings, or booths for polling at elections. Retford had a particularly
bad reputation for the conduct of parliamentary elections, due to the
small number of voters, thus making it easier for corruption and
bribery to take place. 'Rotten' and 'pocket' boroughs of course existed
elsewhere until the system of representation was altered by the Reform
Act of 1832. In Retford's case however the situation became so bad that
after an election in 1826 a parliamentary committee was set up because
of the actions of a 'lawless and infuriated mob'. As a result, Retford
ceased to be a parliamentary borough in its own right and the electors
were compelled to become part of a larger constituency covering the
north of the county.

Eventually, the Broad Stone together with other obstructions in the
Market Place were removed, the Stone to its present site.

Places of Interest in the Neighbourhood
Free Board and Lodging (Worksop)
Reflections of Former Glory (Shireoaks)

75 Free Board and Lodging

Position: Worksop
O.S. Map: Mansfield & Worksop area: Sheet No. 120: 1/50,000
Map Ref: SK 590/788
Access: The Priory Gatehouse is on the B.6040 road, 2 miles west from
the junction with the A.57 road.

The Church of St. Cuthbert and Mary at Worksop, now also known as
Worksop Priory, was originally known as Radford Priory as it stood in
a separate township of that name which in later years became incorporated in the borough of Worksop. William de Lovetot founded a
monastery here in 1103 occupied by Augustinian Canons.

In 1314 the Archbishop of York gave the Priory permission to fell 200

The Priory Gatehouse, Worksop.

oak trees in Sherwood Forest and it is thought these were used to build the Gatehouse. At first the building only contained the main hall on the first floor, with smaller rooms over the archway. A porch and shrine chapel were added later on the south-east corner of the building.

The Gatehouse became a secular and ecclesiastical meeting point as it was adjacent to the market cross, a market and fair having been granted in 1296. It was the custom to grant sanctuary in the main hall to any stranger who presented himself. He had to be received "as if Christ himself" and given food and shelter for three days without having to give his name. At the dissolution of the monasteries in 1539, most of the monastic buildings were pulled down, but the Gatehouse survived. The road through the archway was made a public thoroughfare, which it remained until the nineteenth century.

It is claimed that in 1628, when the main hall was used as a school that it was the first elementary school in England. It continued to be used as a school until.the 1960's, being known as the 'Abbeygate' in the nineteenth century, when it was a school for poor boys, supported by voluntary subscriptions.

The Gatehouse has undergone some alterations over the years. At one time there was a blacksmith's shop attached to the south-east of the building and a thatched parsonage on the east side. After serious vandalism took place in 1813, work of restoration was carried out. Further restoration was undertaken in 1891, when the road through the arch was closed and a new one at the side of the Gatehouse was built. The decorative south front with its figures and niches formed the model for the Clipstone Archway (see No.62).

Places of Interest in the Neighbourhood
An Early Disinfecting Station (Retford)
Reflections of Former Glory (Shireoaks)

76 Reflections of Former Glory

Position: Shireoaks, near Worksop
O.S. Map: Mansfield & Worksop area: Sheet No. 120: 1/50,000
Map Ref: SK 551/805
Access: About 50 yards along the road marked to Thorpe Salvin is a
signed footpath. This continues past the 'Hewett Arms', through a gate
and a right-angled bend.

From the above-mentioned footpath one can see Shireoaks Hall in one
direction and the canal in the other direction. This is no ordinary canal,
as it only stretches for about half a mile and is ornamental and not
intended for narrow or other boats. The water gardens of which the
canal was part were constructed about 1690 by the then owner of
Shireoaks Hall, Sir Thomas Hewett.

   The water gardens which he laid out were on a magnificent scale but
after the death of the last Hewett in 1811 the Hall and estate were sold
and the water gardens were neglected. A visitor in 1825 commented on
their desolate appearance. Fortunately the present owners of the Hall
have done much to renovate both the Hall and the remains of the gardens.

   The original lay-out of the gardens had a geometrical precision and
were designed as a striking feature of the view from the house. Half
hidden today in a wood is the large circular stone-lined basin, fed from
a spring. The water then flowed along in a series of thirty-four cascades
with twelve oval and circular ponds which ended in the canal. Avenues
of yews and lime trees flanked the sides. Although much of the original
glory has disappeared, the remains are carefully preserved to provide
the natural habitat of the flora and fauna.

Places of Interest in the Neighbourhood
Free Board and Lodging (Worksop)
An Early Disinfecting Station (Retford)

77 From Nottinghamshire to New England

Position: Scrooby, 7 miles north of Retford
O.S. Map: Sheffield & Doncaster: Sheet No. 111: 1/50,000
Map Ref: SK 651/903
Access: Scrooby is on the A.638 road and the 'Pilgrim Fathers' public house is on the west side of the road.

Scrooby today is a quiet and peaceful village, like a number of similar places in this thinly populated area of North Nottinghamshire. When William Brewster was born here in the reign of the first Queen Elizabeth it was of considerable importance, for it was situated on the Great North Road and for centuries had been one of the principal seats of the Archbishops of York. There is now no trace of the former palace which was demolished at the beginning of the eighteenth century.

Nor is there any proven survivals of the house where William Brewster was born and lived. His father was Master of the Queens Post, an important job which entailed escorting official visitors and royal messages between Tuxford in the south and Doncaster in the north. From the income of this post he was able to send his son to Cambridge University, entering Peterhouse College in 1580. It was here that he became interested in the Separatist movement for independent religious freedom, a movement frowned on by the established church. When he returned to Scrooby, he succeeded his father as Master of the Post for 17 years. Here he was joined by two other men, the Reverend Richard Clyfton who was deprived of his living at nearby Babworth and William Bradford, from Austerfield just over the Yorkshire border. They formed a Separatist church at Scrooby in 1606. This was to lead to the decision a year later by Brewster and a number of his friends to leave England to escape religious persecution. They first went to Holland and in 1620 crossed the Atlantic in the *Mayflower* to found the colony of New England.

Even if the only reminder in Scrooby of this historic event is the sign of the Pilgrims Fathers inn, a visit to the village can be a rewarding one. There is a splendid ancient mill on the little River Ryton down which at night the small band of women and children made their way from Scrooby to join the men who walked over land to the Humber.

Places of Interest in the Neighbourhood
A Reminder of a Handsome Mansion (Blyth)

78 A Reminder of a Handsome Mansion

Position: Blyth
O.S. Map: Mansfield & Worksop area: Sheet No. 120: 1/50,000
Map Ref: SK 622/871
Access: Blyth is on the A.634 road, 500 yards west of the A.1 road.

The elegant wrought iron gateway, just a few yards south of the church, is all that remains of Blyth Hall, which was demolished in 1972. The Hall was built in 1684/5 for Edward Mellish, a member of a London family which moved north in the seventeenth century. Edward died unmarried in 1703 and the estate was left to a cousin, Joseph. His son William carried out a number of improvements to the Hall and to the surrounding countryside. He had a river made, four miles long, to drain the meadows, planted woods and erected farm houses, cottages and a bridge.

White's *Directory of Nottinghamshire* for 1832 commented: "Little did this spirited gentleman imagine, whilst making these improvements, that his extensive estate was so soon to pass from his family by the improvidence of his son, Charles Mellish". The latter, although an educated man with literary tastes "became at length so enamoured of the company of royalty, and so addicted to the vices of the turf and the fashionable gaming table that he was obliged to sell the Blyth Hall Estate."

After remaining in the ownership of two succeeding families for over a hundred years, the Hall was unoccupied for many years, becoming almost derelict before it was demolished.

Places of Interest in the Neighbourhood
From Nottinghamshire to New England (Scrooby)
Light at the End of a Tunnel (Drakeholes)
A Clean Living Squire (Wiseton)

79 Light at the End of a Tunnel

Position: Drakeholes, near Bawtry
O.S. Map: Doncaster: Sheet No. 111: 1/50,000
Map Ref: SK 707/904
Access: Drakeholes' canal basin and tunnel are on the A.631 road, 4
miles east of Bawtry.

Chesterfield in Derbyshire gives its name to the canal which starts there
and flows 45 miles eastwards to join the River Trent at West Stockwith.
However, 28 of those miles are in Nottinghamshire.

The canal was opened in 1777 so that the lead and iron mined in
Derbyshire could be distributed more easily. Until then they had to be
taken by primitive roads, as far as Bawtry. There they were shipped
along the River Idle Navigation to West Stockwith. This was a far from

The Chesterfield Canal at Drakeholes.

satisfactory state of affairs as the roads would be difficult in winter, whilst the River Idle was subject to floods in winter and to low levels in dry summers.

After the Duke of Bridgewater had shown the advantages of a canal being used to transport coal cheaply, a number of merchants and land-owners interested in trade in North Nottinghamshire and Derbyshire decided to promote a Parliamentary Bill to allow them to build a similar canal. The Bill received the Royal Assent in 1771 and James Brindley, who had already established his reputation as a canal engineer, was engaged to carry out the work.

The route of the canal was not far from the River Idle as far as Retford and a few miles beyond. From Wiseton however the ground rose rather steeply and the River Idle flowed in a long detour along the flatter land. Accordingly Brindley planned a tunnel at Drakeholes under the Bawtry to Gainsborough road. Once through the tunnel, the canal could strike an almost straight line to West Stockwith.

A contract to build the tunnel in twenty weeks was let, with a penalty of £1 per week for every week's delay. The tunnel was 154 yards long and 15 feet 6 inches high and was cut through solid sandstone, not needing a brick lining. The towpath had to go over the hill and the boats had to be shafted through the tunnel, as it was far too high for the 'legging' method possible in lower tunnels. Marks made by shafting can be seen in the tunnel. A basin and wharf were built which brought prosperity to the White Swan Inn nearby, now known as the Griff Inn.

The canal, like those in the rest of the country, ceased to be of commercial use when railways were established and although the Chesterfield Canal enjoyed a new lease of life during the 1939-45 War, traffic ceased in the mid-1950's. Now however thanks to the enthusiasm and hard work of canal lovers, the Chesterfield Canal is open as far as Worksop for leisure purposes.

Places of Interest in the Neighbourhood
A Reminder of a Handsome Mansion (Blyth)
From Nottinghamshire to New England (Scrooby)
A Clean Living Squire (Wiseton)

80 A Clean Living Squire

Position: Wiseton, near Bawtry
O.S. Map: Mansfield & Worksop area: Sheet No. 120: 1/50,000
Map Ref: SK 718/899
Access: Wiseton is a mile south-west of the junction of the A.631 road
and the B.6045 road.

The unspoilt village of Wiseton had an eighteenth century Hall until
1960 when it was demolished. Two ancillary buildings have however
remained. Approaching the village from the west one sees the long red-
brick block of stables. At the eastern end is a picturesque group of
cottages with colourful gardens. These were formerly the laundry for
the Hall.

Wiseton and its surroundings owe much of their appearance to the
development carried out in the eighteenth century by Jonathan
Acklom. In addition to the Hall he was responsible for the inn at
Drakeholes (see No. 79) and for two farmhouses, all built in Palladian
fashion and occupying prominent positions on hill-tops. The estate
passed in the nineteenth century to the Laycock family, in whose
possession it remained until 1960. The last of the line was General
'Lucky' Laycock who was Governor of Malta in the 1939-45 war.

Places of Interest in the Neighbourhood
From Nottinghamshire to New England (Scrooby)
A Reminder of a Handsome Mansion (Blyth)
Light at the End of a Tunnel (Drakeholes)

The former laundry at Wiseton.

Index

Places by page number

The Curiosities of England

The following titles in the series have already been published and can be ordered at all bookshops, or in case of difficulties direct from the publishers.